Designing Web APIs
Building APIs That Developers Love

*Brenda Jin, Saurabh Sahni,
and Amir Shevat*

Beijing · Boston · Farnham · Sebastopol · Tokyo

Designing Web APIs

by Brenda Jin, Saurabh Sahni, and Amir Shevat

Copyright © 2018 Brenda Jin, Saurabh Sahni, and Amir Shevat. All rights reserved.

Published by O'Reilly Media, Inc., 1005 Gravenstein Highway North, Sebastopol, CA 95472.

O'Reilly books may be purchased for educational, business, or sales promotional use. Online editions are also available for most titles (*http://oreilly.com/safari*). For more information, contact our corporate/institutional sales department: 800-998-9938 or *corporate@oreilly.com*.

Acquisitions Editor: Mary Treseler	**Indexer:** Ellen Troutman
Development Editor: Angela Rufino	**Interior Designer:** David Futato
Production Editor: Justin Billing	**Cover Designer:** Karen Montgomery
Copyeditor: Octal Publishing, Inc.	**Illustrator:** Rebecca Demarest
Proofreader: Rachel Head	

September 2018:   First Edition

Revision History for the First Edition
2018-08-28:   First Release

See *http://oreilly.com/catalog/errata.csp?isbn=9781492026921* for release details.

978-1-492-02692-1

[LSI]

Table of Contents

Preface

Building a popular developer platform with an API that is used by millions of developers is one of the most challenging and exciting endeavors you can undertake in your software career. In this book, you'll learn how to do that.

APIs are at the core of modern software development. They tackle a basic developer challenge: how can I, as a software engineer, expose the code I've written to other developers to use and innovate with? Building software in the modern world is very much like building with LEGO bricks. As a developer you have access to a vast set of APIs that expose services such as payments, communication, authorization and authentication, and so forth. When building new software, your job as a software engineer is to use these APIs to compose your new product, reusing code that others built in order to save time and avoid reinventing the wheel.

Many software engineers who enjoyed playing with LEGOs as kids still love to play with them today. And who wouldn't? It's fun, and you get to build useful stuff with awesome colorful pieces that connect to one another seamlessly. But what if you could build the LEGO itself? Wouldn't it be great if you could invent not only new LEGO kits, but also the LEGO parts themselves, and let others innovate with them? When building your own API, you are in effect creating your own LEGO parts for other developers to use.

APIs are not a new concept in computer science—in the '60s, developers began to build standard libraries for the first procedural languages and share these with other developers. These developers could use the standard functionality of these libraries without knowing their internal code.

Then, in the '70s and '80s, with the emergence of network-connected computers, came the first network APIs that exposed services developers could consume through Remote Procedure Calls (RPCs). With RPCs, developers could expose their functionality over the network and call remote libraries as if they were local. Programming languages like Java provided further abstraction and complexity, with messaging middleware servers that listed and orchestrated these remote services.

During the '90s, with the emergence of the internet, many companies wanted to standardize the way we build and expose APIs. Standards such as the Common Object Request Broker Architecture (CORBA), the Component Object Model (COM) and Distributed Component Object Model (DCOM) by Microsoft, and many others sought to become the de facto way to expose services over the web. The problem was that most of these standards were complex to manage, mandated similar programming languages on both sides of the network, and sometimes required the local installation of part of the remote service (commonly called a _stub_) in order to access it. It was a mess; the dream of interoperability soon became a nightmare of configurations and constraints.

In the late '90s and early '00s came more open and standard ways of accessing remote services over the web (web APIs). First with the Simple Object Access Protocol (SOAP) and Extensible Markup Language (XML), and then with Representative State Transfer (REST) and JavaScript Object Notation (JSON), accessing services became easier and more standardized without dependencies on client-side code or programming language. We cover the more popular and useful of these methods in this book.

One by one, every tech company began exposing useful services through APIs—from the early days of the Amazon Affiliate API (2002), to the Flickr API (2004), the Google Maps API (2005), and the Yahoo! Pipes API (2007), there are now thousands of APIs exposing every service imaginable, from image manipulation to artificial intelligence. Developers can call these and create new products that are a composition of multiple APIs, just like building with LEGO bricks.

Although APIs have become a commodity and using them an easy task, building an API is still an art form. Do not take this challenge lightly; building a solid API is not easy. APIs should be brilliantly simple and highly interoperable—like with LEGO, each part from any kit should work well with every other piece in any other kit. APIs should also be accompanied by developer programs and resources to help developers adopt them. Building a solid API is just the first step; you also need to create and support a thriving ecosystem of developers. We cover these challenges in the last part of this book.

We wrote this book because we realized that over the course of our careers we had followed similar processes and made similar decisions, processes, and optimizations for many APIs, but these guidelines had not been compiled into a single authoritative resource. We could each point to blog posts or articles here and there about separate topics, but there wasn't one place that described how to design for the evolution and growth of web APIs and their ecosystems. With this book, we hope to put at your fingertips all the tools that we've created and discovered over the course of our careers building APIs. Having access to this skill set is very valuable. It can be the difference between the success and failure of your business or technology, and it can be the unique advantage that will drive your career.

How This Book Is Organized

This book comprises three major parts:

Theory (Chapters 1–4)
> Here we cover the basic concepts of building an API, review different API patterns, and discuss different aspects of a good API.

Practice (Chapters 5–7)
> In these chapters, we talk about how to actually design an API and manage its operation in production.

Developer Love (Chapters 8–11)
> In this section, we go beyond designing an API and show you how to build a thriving developer ecosystem around your API.

Also included in this book are case studies (lessons from Stripe, Slack, Twitch, Microsoft, Uber, GitHub, Facebook, Cloudinary, Oracle, and more!), advice and pro tips from experts in the field, and stories about real-life experiences. In Appendix A, you'll find some handy worksheets, templates, and checklists.

Conventions Used in This Book

The following typographical conventions are used in this book:

Italic
> Indicates new terms, URLs, email addresses, filenames, and file extensions.

`Constant width`
> Used for program listings, as well as within paragraphs to refer to program elements such as variable or function names, databases, data types, environment variables, statements, and keywords.

`Constant width bold`
> Shows commands or other text that should be typed literally by the user.

`Constant width italic`
> Shows text that should be replaced with user-supplied values or by values determined by context.

This element signifies a "Pro Tip."

This element signifies a general note.

This element indicates a warning or caution.

O'Reilly Safari

 *Safari* (formerly Safari Books Online) is a membership-based training and reference platform for enterprise, government, educators, and individuals.

Members have access to thousands of books, training videos, Learning Paths, interactive tutorials, and curated playlists from over 250 publishers, including O'Reilly Media, Harvard Business Review, Prentice Hall Professional, Addison-Wesley Professional, Microsoft Press, Sams, Que, Peachpit Press, Adobe, Focal Press, Cisco Press, John Wiley & Sons, Syngress, Morgan Kaufmann, IBM Redbooks, Packt, Adobe Press, FT Press, Apress, Manning, New Riders, McGraw-Hill, Jones & Bartlett, and Course Technology, among others.

For more information, please visit *http://oreilly.com/safari*.

How to Contact Us

Please address comments and questions concerning this book to the publisher:

O'Reilly Media, Inc.
1005 Gravenstein Highway North
Sebastopol, CA 95472
800-998-9938 (in the United States or Canada)
707-829-0515 (international or local)
707-829-0104 (fax)

We have a web page for this book, where we list errata, examples, and any additional information. You can access this page at *https://bit.ly/designing-web-apis*.

To comment or ask technical questions about this book, send email to *bookquestions@oreilly.com*.

For more information about our books, courses, conferences, and news, see our website at *http://www.oreilly.com*.

Find us on Facebook: *http://facebook.com/oreilly*

Follow us on Twitter: *http://twitter.com/oreillymedia*

Watch us on YouTube: *http://www.youtube.com/oreillymedia*

Acknowledgments

Thanks to our families, whose love and support have made this book possible.

Special thanks to our technical reviewers Bilal Aijazi, James Higgenbotham, Jenny Donnelly, Margaret Le, and Melissa Khuat.

Thank you as well to Eric Conlon, Or Weis, Taylor Singletary, and Zoe Madden-Wood, who provided additional comments and feedback.

Finally, thank you to all the folks who participated in interviews and case studies and otherwise helped shape this book:

- Bilal Aijazi, CTO at Polly
- Chris Messina, developer experience lead at Uber
- Desiree Motamedi Ward, head of developer product marketing at Facebook
- Ido Green, developer advocate at Google
- Kyle Daigle, director of ecosystem engineering at GitHub
- Ran Rubinstein, VP of solutions at Cloudinary
- Romain Huet, head of developer relations at Stripe
- Ron Reiter, senior director of engineering at Oracle
- Taylor Singletary, lead content writer at Slack
- Yochay Kiriaty, Azure principal program manager at Microsoft

CHAPTER 1

What's an API?

"What's an API?" When a new programmer asks this question, they typically get the answer, "an application programming interface."

But APIs are so much more than their name suggests—and to understand and unleash their value, we must focus on the keyword *interface*.

An API is the interface that a software program presents to other programs, to humans, and, in the case of web APIs, to the world via the Internet. An API's design belies much about the program behind it—business model, product features, the occasional bug. Although APIs are designed to work with other programs, they're mostly intended to be understood and used by *humans* writing those other programs.

APIs are the building blocks that allow interoperability for major business platforms on the web. APIs are how identity is created and maintained across cloud software accounts, from your corporate email address to your collaborative design software to the web applications that help you order pizza delivery. APIs are how weather forecast data is shared from a reputable source like the National Weather Service to hundreds of software apps that specialize in its presentation. APIs process your credit cards and enable companies to seamlessly collect your money without worrying about the minutiae of financial technology and its corresponding laws and regulations.

More and more, APIs are a key component of scalable and successful internet companies like Amazon, Stripe, Google, and Facebook. For companies looking to create a business platform that expands the market for everyone, APIs are an important piece of the puzzle.

Designing your first API is just the beginning. This book goes beyond design principles for your first API and dives into how to develop and grow an API alongside your business. With the right choices, your API will stand the test of time.

Why Do We Need APIs?

APIs have emerged out of a need to exchange information with providers of data who are equipped to solve specific problems, so folks at other companies don't have to spend time solving those problems themselves. For example, you might want to embed an interactive map on a web page without reinventing Google Maps. You might want to have a user sign in without having to reinvent Facebook Login. Or, you might want to create a chatbot that occasionally interacts with users without having to build a real-time messaging system.

In all of these cases, supplementary features and products are created using data or interactions from a specialized platform. APIs enable businesses to develop unique products quickly. Rather than reinventing the wheel, startups are able to differentiate their product offerings while taking advantage of existing technologies and tapping into other ecosystems.

Who Are Our Users?

> *None of the theory matters if you're not focused on building the right thing for the right customer.*
> —Bilal Aijazi, CTO at Polly

When building any product, it is a good idea to focus on the customer first. This is also very important when designing an API. In Chapter 8, we talk about different types of developers and use cases as well as strategies to engage with them and give them value. It is important that you understand who your developers are, what their needs are, and why they are using your API. Focusing on developers prevents you from building APIs that no one wants to use or that do not fit the usage requirements of your developers.

Because changing an API's design is very difficult after the fact, it is important that you specify your API and validate it long before you start to implement it. The cost of switching from one API design to another is extremely high for most developers.

Here are some examples of developer use cases for an image upload and storage API:

- Lisa is a web developer in a startup that sells art, and she needs an easy way for the artists to upload and show photos of their work.
- Ben is a backend enterprise developer who needs to store receipts coming from the expense system into his audit and policy solution.
- Jane is a frontend developer who wants to integrate real-time customer support chat onto her company's website.

These are just a few examples, each with unique hidden requirements and needs. If you do not address your developers' needs, your API will not be successful.

In the next section, we talk about high-level use cases that can have an impact on the design of your API, but the more granular you can be with your use cases and the better you understand your developers, the better you can serve them.

The Business Case for APIs

It's no secret that the web powers a large portion of new product innovation and the technology market today. As a result, APIs are more important than ever in creating a business, and there are many models for incorporating them into a product. In some cases, an API will lead to direct profit and monetization (via profit share models, subscription fees, or usage fees). But there are also many other reasons you might want to create an API. APIs might support your company's overall product strategy. They might be a critical piece of the puzzle for integrating third-party services with your company's product. APIs might be part of a strategy to incentivize others to build supplemental products in which the developer of the main product is unwilling or unable to invest. APIs might also be a way to generate leads, create new distribution channels for a product, or upsell products. For more information on these strategies, see John Musser's presentation on API business models (*https://www.slideshare.net/jmusser/j-musser-apibizmodels2013*).

An API must be aligned with the core business, as is the case with many software as a service (SaaS) companies. Notable examples are GitHub, Salesforce, and Stripe. Sometimes, the products built on these APIs are referred to as "service integrations." Consumer APIs work well if there is a critical mass of user-generated content, such as with Facebook and Flickr's photo-sharing capabilities. Although there are many reasons to create an API and launch a developer platform, there is also a clear reason *not* to create a developer platform—when the API strategy is not aligned with the core business. For example, if the product's main revenue stream is advertisements, APIs that enable alternative "clients" for the product will drive traffic away from the experience where the ads are hosted. That will take away from revenue share, as was the case with the Twitter API.

Monetization and business incentives aside, let's take a more detailed look at the following ways that some companies have structured their API development:

- APIs for internal developers first, external developers second
- APIs for external developers first, internal developers second
- APIs as the product

APIs for Internal Developers First, External Developers Second

Some companies build their APIs for internal developers first and then release them to external developers. There could be a number of motivations for this. One reason might be that the company sees potential value in adding an external API. This could create a developer ecosystem, drive new demand for the company's product, or enable other companies to build products that the company itself does not want to build.

To take a look at a specific instance, let's explore how Slack's API started—as an API for Slack's web, native desktop, and mobile clients to display a messaging interface. Although Slack originally created its APIs for its internal developers, something else happened as the company grew: a handful of "integrations" with important business software became a key piece of the puzzle for Slack's growth and development as communication software. Instead of building bespoke apps to integrate its offering with other companies, Slack launched its Developer Platform and a suite of products for third-party developers to build their own apps, both at established companies and at new startups.

This move on Slack's part helped to grow the ecosystem for apps that integrate with Slack's messaging platform. It also meant that users of Slack who also used other business software could seamlessly collaborate where communication was already happening in the Slack messaging client.

The advantage to Slack's APIs at the time of its Developer Platform launch was that the APIs were already tested and well used by internal developers. The disadvantages to this approach showed up over time as the needs of external developers drifted apart from the needs of internal developers. Internal developers needed flexibility to create new experiences for end users of the messaging client, from new types of shared channels, files, and messages, to other increasingly complex communication experiences. Meanwhile, third-party developers were no longer creating replacement client user interfaces (UIs) for Slack—they started to create powerful business applications and tools that were designed for workflows rather than message display. External developers also required stability, and the tension between API backward compatibility and the need to change the API for new product features had a cost on project velocity within Slack.

APIs for External Developers First, Internal Developers Second

Some companies create APIs for external stakeholders first and then release them to internal stakeholders. That's how GitHub has operated since the beginning. Let's take a look at how and why GitHub developed its API and how its developer audience has affected the evolution of the API.

In the beginning, GitHub's API audience was primarily external developers who wanted to gain programmatic access to their own data. Shortly after the initial release of their API, small businesses began to form around GitHub's API. These businesses were creating developer tools and selling them to GitHub's users.

Since then, GitHub has expanded its API offering significantly. It has built an API that serves both individuals who want to create their own personal projects or workflows and teams that want to collaborate to build bot scripts or workflow tools that integrate with GitHub. These teams, called *integrators*, build developer tools, connect users with GitHub's platform, and sell these tools to mutual customers.

When it came time for GitHub to build its GraphQL API, third-party developers were the first consumers. GraphQL is a query interface for web APIs. Although it isn't the first such interface, it gained a bit of buzz prior to the writing of this book due to its implementation by Facebook, a well-known API provider, and its adoption by GitHub, another well-known API provider. After third-party developers began to use GitHub's new GraphQL API, internal GitHub developers also adopted it to power the GitHub web UI and client applications.

In GitHub's case, the API had a clear intention to serve external stakeholders first and then eventually evolved to serve internal developers as well. One advantage to this approach is that the API can be customized to serve external developers, rather than straddling two audiences. As GitHub's API evolved, it was able to annotate its JSON responses with more and more data that developers needed. Eventually, the payloads were so large that GitHub implemented GraphQL so that developers could specify the fields they wanted with the queries. One disadvantage to this approach in the case of GraphQL is that due to the flexibility that GraphQL gives developers, performance bottlenecks that emerge are spread across a variety of access patterns. This can make troubleshooting tricker than when working with a single endpoint at a time, for example in the case of REST.

 For more details on GraphQL, see Chapter 2.

APIs as the Product

For some companies, the API *is* the product. Such is the case with Stripe and Twilio. Stripe provides APIs for payment processing on the internet. Twilio provides APIs for communication via SMS, voice, and messaging. In the case of these two companies, building an API is 100% aligned with a single-product audience. The API is the product, and the entire business aligns behind building a seamless interface for customers. As far as managing APIs and meeting user needs, the API as the product is the most straightforward company arrangement possible.

What Makes an API Great?

We asked industry experts this question, and the answers we received boiled down to whether the API achieves what it is supposed to do. To delve into the aspects that contribute to an API's usability, we will not only explore aspects of designing and scaling APIs, but also the support and ecosystems that enable developers to use APIs.

Expert Advice

A good API may come down to the problem you're trying to solve and how valuable solving it is. You may be willing to use a confusing, inconsistent, poorly documented API if it means you're getting access to a unique dataset or complex functionality. Otherwise, good APIs tend to offer clarity (of purpose, design, and context), flexibility (ability to be adapted to different use cases), power (completeness of the solution offered), hackability (ability to pick up quickly through iteration and experimentation), and documentation.

—Chris Messina, developer experience lead at Uber

Usability, scalability, and performance are some of the aspects that make a good API. We cover many of these topics in Chapters 2 through 4 of this book. Documentation and developer resources are also important to setting users up for success. We cover those in Chapters 7 through 9. Because it is impossible to optimize an API for all factors, the implementation team must make tough decisions about what is most important for the end user. We teach you how to build a strategy to address this in Chapter 7.

One more thing to consider is how a great API will stand the test of time. Change is difficult and inevitable. APIs are flexible platforms that connect businesses, and the rate of change is variable. In large-enterprise contexts, the rate of change is slower than in small start-ups that have not yet found *product–market fit*. But sometimes, these small startups provide invaluable services via APIs that enterprises must use. In Chapter 5, you also learn about how to design APIs to stand the test of time and change.

Closing Thoughts

In summary, APIs are an important component of modern tech products, and there are many ways to structure a business using them. In Chapter 2, we give you an overview of API design paradigms.

API Paradigms

Picking the right API paradigm is important. An API paradigm defines the interface exposing backend data of a service to other applications. When starting out with APIs, organizations do not always consider all the factors that will make an API successful. As a result, there isn't enough room built in to add the features they want later on. This can also happen when the organization or product changes over time. Unfortunately, after there are developers using it, changing an API is difficult (if not impossible). To save time, effort and headaches—and to leave room for new and exciting features— it's worthwhile to give some thought to protocols, patterns, and a few best practices before you get started. This will help you design an API that allows you to make the changes you want in the future.

Over the years, multiple API paradigms have emerged. REST, RPC, GraphQL, WebHooks, and WebSockets are some of the most popular standards today. In this chapter, we dive into these different paradigms.

Request–Response APIs

Request–response APIs typically expose an interface through an HTTP-based web server. APIs define a set of endpoints. Clients make HTTP requests for data to those endpoints and the server returns responses. The response is typically sent back as JSON or XML. There are three common paradigms used by services to expose request–response APIs: REST, RPC, and GraphQL. We look into each of them in the subsections that follow.

Representational State Transfer

Representational State Transfer (REST) is the most popular choice for API development lately. The REST paradigm is used by providers like Google, Stripe, Twitter, and GitHub. REST is all about *resources*. A resource is an entity that can be identified, named, addressed, or handled on the web. REST APIs expose data as resources and use standard HTTP methods to represent Create, Read, Update, and Delete (CRUD) transactions against these resources. For instance, Stripe's API represents customers, charges, balance, refunds, events, files, and payouts as resources.

Here are some general rules REST APIs follow:

- Resources are part of URLs, like /users.

- For each resource, two URLs are generally implemented: one for the collection, like /users, and one for a specific element, like /users/U123.

- Nouns are used instead of verbs for resources. For example, instead of /getUserInfo/U123, use /users/U123.

- HTTP methods like GET, POST, UPDATE, and DELETE inform the server about the action to be performed. Different HTTP methods invoked on the same URL provide different functionality:

  Create
  > Use POST for creating new resources.

  Read
  > Use GET for reading resources. GET requests never, ever change the state of the resource. They have no side effects; the GET method has a read-only semantic. GET is idempotent. Consequently, you can cache the calls perfectly.

  Update
  > Use PUT for replacing a resource and PATCH for partial updates for existing resources.

  Delete
  > Use DELETE for deleting existing resources.

- Standard HTTP response status codes are returned by the server indicating success or failure. Generally, codes in the 2XX range indicate success, 3XX codes indicate a resource has moved, and codes in the 4XX range indicate a client-side error (like a missing required parameter or too many requests). Codes in the 5XX range indicate server-side errors.

- REST APIs might return JSON or XML responses. That said, due to its simplicity and ease of use with JavaScript, JSON has become the standard for modern APIs. (XML and other formats might still be supported to make adoption easy for clients that are already working with those formats using similar APIs.)

Table 2-1 shows how HTTP methods are typically used in REST APIs, and Examples 2-1 and 2-2 show some example HTTP requests.

Table 2-1. CRUD operations, HTTP verbs, and REST conventions

Operation	HTTP verb	URL: /users	URL: /users/U123
Create	POST	Create a new user	Not applicable
Read	GET	List all users	Retrieve user U123
Update	PUT or PATCH	Batch update users	Update user U123
Delete	DELETE	Delete all users	Delete user U123

Example 2-1. HTTP request to retrieve a charge from the Stripe API

```
GET /v1/charges/ch_CWyutlXs9pZyfD
HOST api.stripe.com
Authorization: Bearer YNoJ1Yq64iCBhzfL9HNO00fzVrsEjtVl
```

Example 2-2. HTTP request to create a charge from the Stripe API

```
POST /v1/charges/ch_CWyutlXs9pZyfD
HOST api.stripe.com
Content-Type: application/x-www-form-urlencoded
Authorization: Bearer YNoJ1Yq64iCBhzfL9HNO00fzVrsEjtVl

amount=2000&currency=usd
```

Showing relationships

A resource that exists only within another resource can be better represented as a subresource instead of a top-level resource in the URL. This makes the relationship clear for the developers using the API.

For instance, the GitHub API uses subresources to represent relationships in various APIs:

```
POST /repos/:owner/:repo/issues
```
Create an issue.

```
GET /repos/:owner/:repo/issues/:number
```
Retrieve an issue.

```
GET /repos/:owner/:repo/issues
```
List all issues.

```
PATCH /repos/:owner/:repo/issues/:number
```
Edit an issue.

Non-CRUD operations

Beyond the typical CRUD operations that we just looked at, REST APIs might sometimes need to represent non-CRUD operations. The following approaches are commonly used in that case:

- Render an action as part of a field of a resource. For example, as shown in Example 2-3, GitHub's API uses `"archived"` as an input parameter to the repo edit API to represent archiving a repository action.

- Treat an action like a subresource. The GitHub API uses this pattern for locking and unlocking an issue. `PUT /repos/:owner/:repo/issues/:number/lock` locks an issue.

- Some operations, such as search, are even more difficult to fit in the REST paradigm. A typical practice in that case is to use just the action verb in the API URL. `GET /search/code?q=:query:` finds files in GitHub matching the given query.

Example 2-3. HTTP request to archive a GitHub repository

```
PATCH /repos/saurabhsahni/Hacks
HOST api.github.com
Content-Type: application/json
Authorization: token OAUTH-TOKEN

{
  "archived": true
}
```

Remote Procedure Call

Remote Procedure Call (RPC) is one of the simplest API paradigms, in which a client executes a block of code on another server. Whereas REST is about resources, RPC is about *actions*. Clients typically pass a method name and arguments to a server and receive back JSON or XML.

RPC APIs generally follow two simple rules:

- The endpoints contain the name of the operation to be executed.
- API calls are made with the HTTP verb that is most appropriate: GET for read-only requests and POST for others.

RPC style works great for APIs that expose a variety of actions that might have more nuances and complications than can be encapsulated with CRUD or for which there are side effects unrelated to the "resource" at hand. RPC-style APIs also accommodate complicated resource models or actions upon multiple types of resources.

One notable example of an RPC-style web API is Slack's API. Example 2-4 demonstrates an example of a POST request to Slack's conversations.archive RPC API.

Example 2-4. HTTP request to Slack's API

```
POST /api/conversations.archive
HOST slack.com
Content-Type: application/x-www-form-urlencoded
Authorization: Bearer xoxp-1650112-jgc2asDae

channel=C01234
```

Slack's Conversations API (Figure 2-1) allows several actions, like archive, join, kick, leave, and rename. Although in this case there *is* a clear "resource," not all of these actions would fit into the REST pattern nicely. Additionally, there are other actions, such as posting a message with chat.postMessage, which have complex relationships with message resources, attachment resources, and visibility settings within the web client.

Conversations API methods

Method	Description
conversations.archive	Archives a conversation.
conversations.close	Closes a direct message or multi-person direct message.
conversations.create	Initiates a public or private channel-based conversation
conversations.history	Fetches a conversation's history of messages and events.
conversations.info	Retrieve information about a conversation.
conversations.invite	Invites users to a channel.
conversations.join	Joins an existing conversation.
conversations.kick	Removes a user from a conversation.
conversations.leave	Leaves a conversation.
conversations.list	Lists all channels in a Slack team.
conversations.members	Retrieve members of a conversation.
conversations.open	Opens or resumes a direct message or multi-person direct message.

Figure 2-1. RPC-style Slack API methods

RPC-style APIs are not exclusive to HTTP. There are other high-performance protocols that are available for RPC-style APIs, including Apache Thrift (*https://thrift.apache.org/*) and gRPC (*https://grpc.io/docs/guides/index.html*). Although there are JSON options for gRPC, both Thrift and gRPC requests are serialized. Structured data and clearly defined interfaces enable this serialization. Thrift and gRPC also have built-in mechanisms for editing the data structures. We don't explore many examples of either gRPC or Thrift in this book, but we thought they were worth mentioning here.

GraphQL

GraphQL (*http://graphql.org/*) is a query language for APIs that has gained significant traction recently. It was developed internally by Facebook in 2012 before being publicly released in 2015 and has been adopted by API providers like GitHub, Yelp, and Pinterest.

GraphQL allows clients to define the structure of the data required, and the server returns exactly that structure. Examples 2-5 and 2-6 show a GraphQL query to the GitHub API and the response.

Example 2-5. GraphQL query

```
{
  user(login: "saurabhsahni") {
    id
    name
    company
    createdAt
  }
}
```

Example 2-6. Response from GitHub GraphQL API

```
{
  "data": {
    "user": {
      "id": "MDQ6VXNlcjY1MDI5",
      "name": "Saurabh Sahni",
      "company": "Slack",
      "createdAt": "2009-03-19T21:00:06Z"
    }
  }
}
```

Unlike REST and RPC APIs, GraphQL APIs need only a single URL endpoint. Similarly, you do not need different HTTP verbs to describe the operation. Instead, you indicate in the JSON body whether you're performing a query or a mutation, as illustrated in Example 2-7. GraphQL APIs support GET and POST verbs.

Example 2-7. GraphQL API call to GitHub

```
POST /graphql
HOST api.github.com
Content-Type: application/json
Authorization: bearer 2332dg1acf9f502737d5e
   xoxp-16501860787-17163410960-113570727396-7051650

{
  "query": "query { viewer { login }}"
}
```

GraphQL has a few key advantages over REST and RPC:

Saves multiple round trips
GraphQL enables clients to nest queries and fetch data across resources in a single request. Without GraphQL, this might require multiple HTTP calls to the server. This means mobile applications using GraphQL can be quick, even on slow network connections.

Avoids versioning
You can add new fields and types to a GraphQL API without affecting existing queries. Similarly, deprecating existing fields is easier. By doing log analysis, an API provider can figure out which clients are using a field. You can hide deprecated fields from tools and remove them when no clients are using them. With REST and RPC APIs, it's harder to figure out which clients are using a deprecated field, making removal more difficult.

Smaller payload size
REST and RPC APIs often end up responding with data that clients might not ever use. With GraphQL, because clients can exactly specify what they need, the payload sizes can be smaller. GraphQL queries return predictable results while giving clients control over the data that is returned.

Strongly typed
GraphQL is strongly typed. At development time, GraphQL type checking helps in ensuring that a query is syntactically correct and valid. This makes building high-quality, less error-prone clients easy.

Introspection
Although there are external solutions like Swagger that help make exploring REST APIs easy, GraphQL is natively discoverable. It comes with GraphiQL (*https://github.com/graphql/graph iql*), an in-browser IDE for exploring GraphQL. It lets users write, validate, and test GraphQL queries in a browser. Figure 2-2 shows using GraphiQL to explore the GitHub API.

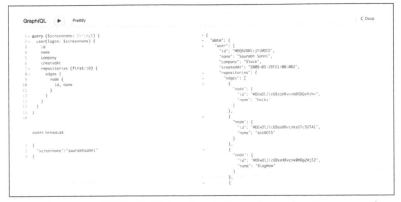

Figure 2-2. GraphiQL: GitHub's GraphQL explorer showing a complex query

Expert Advice

One of the biggest issues GitHub saw was REST payload creep. Over time, you add additional information to a serializer for, say, a repository. It starts small but as you add additional data (maybe you've added a new feature) that primitive ends up producing more and more data until your API responses are enormous.

We've tackled that over the years by creating more endpoints, allowing you to specify you'd like the more verbose response, and by adding more and more caching. But, over time, we realized we were returning a ton of data that our integrators didn't even want. That's one of several reasons we've been investing in our GraphQL API. With GraphQL, you specify a query for just the data you want and we return just that data.

—Kyle Daigle, director of ecosystem engineering at GitHub

Although GraphQL has many advantages, one of its drawbacks is the complexity it adds for the API provider. The server needs to do additional processing to parse complex queries and verify parameters. Optimizing performance of GraphQL queries can be difficult, too. Internally, within a company, it's easy to predict the use cases and debug performance bottlenecks. When working with external developers, those use cases become difficult to understand and optimize for. When opening up GraphQL to third parties, you move the expense of managing multiple incoming requests to composing complicated queries on the backend—depending on the request, the performance and impact to infrastructure can be highly variable.

Table 2-2 summarizes the differences between the various request–response API options.

Table 2-2. Comparison of request–response API paradigms

	REST	RPC	GraphQL
What?	Exposes data as resources and uses standard HTTP methods to represent CRUD operations	Exposes action-based API methods—clients pass method name and arguments	A query language for APIs —clients define the structure of the response
Example services	Stripe, GitHub, Twitter, Google	Slack, Flickr	Facebook, GitHub, Yelp
Example usage	GET /users/<id>	GET /users.get?id=<id>	query ($id: String!) { user(login: $id) { name company createdAt } }
HTTP verbs used	GET, POST, PUT, PATCH, DELETE	GET, POST	GET, POST
Pros	• Standard method name, arguments format, and status codes • Utilizes HTTP features • Easy to maintain	• Easy to understand • Lightweight payloads • High performance	• Saves multiple round trips • Avoids versioning • Smaller payload size • Strongly typed • Built-in introspection
Cons	• Big payloads • Multiple HTTP round trips	• Discovery is difficult • Limited standardization • Can lead to function explosion	• Requires additional query parsing • Backend performance optimization is difficult • Too complicated for a simple API
When to use?	For APIs doing CRUD-like operations	For APIs exposing several actions	When you need querying flexibility; great for providing querying flexibility and maintaining consistency

Event-Driven APIs

With request–response APIs, for services with constantly changing data, the response can quickly become stale. Developers who want to stay up to date with the changes in data often end up *polling* the API. With polling, developers constantly query API endpoints at a predetermined frequency and look for new data.

If developers poll at a low frequency, their apps will not have data about all the events (like a resource being created, updated, or deleted) that occurred since the last poll. However, polling at a high frequency would lead to a huge waste of resources, as most API calls will not return any new data. In one case, Zapier did a study (*https:// zapier.com/engineering/introducing-resthooksorg/*) and found that only about 1.5% of their polling API calls returned new data.

To share data about events in real time, there are three common mechanisms: *WebHooks*, *WebSockets*, and *HTTP Streaming*. We dive deeper into each of them in the subsections that follow.

WebHooks

A WebHook is just a URL that accepts an HTTP POST (or GET, PUT, or DELETE). An API provider implementing WebHooks will simply POST a message to the configured URL when something happens. Unlike with request–response APIs, with WebHooks, you can receive updates in real time. Several API providers, like Slack, Stripe, GitHub, and Zapier, support WebHooks. For instance, if you want to keep track of "channels" in a Slack team with Slack's Web API, you might need to continuously poll the API for new channels. However, as illustrated in Figure 2-3, by configuring a WebHook, you can simply receive a notification whenever a new channel is created.

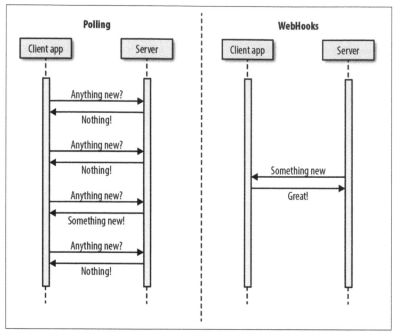

Figure 2-3. Polling versus WebHooks

WebHooks are great for easily sharing real-time data from one server to another server. From an app developer's point of view, it's typically easy to implement WebHooks because it simply requires creating a new HTTP endpoint to receive events (see Figure 2-4). This means that they can generally reuse existing infrastructure. At the same time, supporting WebHooks adds new complexities, including the following:

Failures and retries

To ensure WebHooks are delivered successfully, it's important to build a system that will retry WebHook delivery on errors. Slack built a system that retries failed deliveries up to three times: once immediately, and then one minute later, and finally five minutes later. Further, if the endpoint continues to return errors for 95% of requests, Slack stops sending events to that Web-Hook endpoint and notifies the developer.

Security

Although there are standard ways of making REST API calls secure, security for WebHooks is still evolving. With Web-Hooks, the onus is on app developers to ensure that they've received a legitimate WebHook. That often leads to developers using unverified WebHooks. There are some common patterns that most API providers follow to secure WebHooks, which we discuss in Chapter 3.

Firewalls

Applications running behind firewalls can access APIs over HTTP, but they are unable to receive inbound traffic. For such applications, utilizing WebHooks is difficult and often not possible.

Noise

Typically, each WebHook call represents one single event. When there are thousands of events happening in a short time that need to be sent via a single WebHook, it can be noisy.

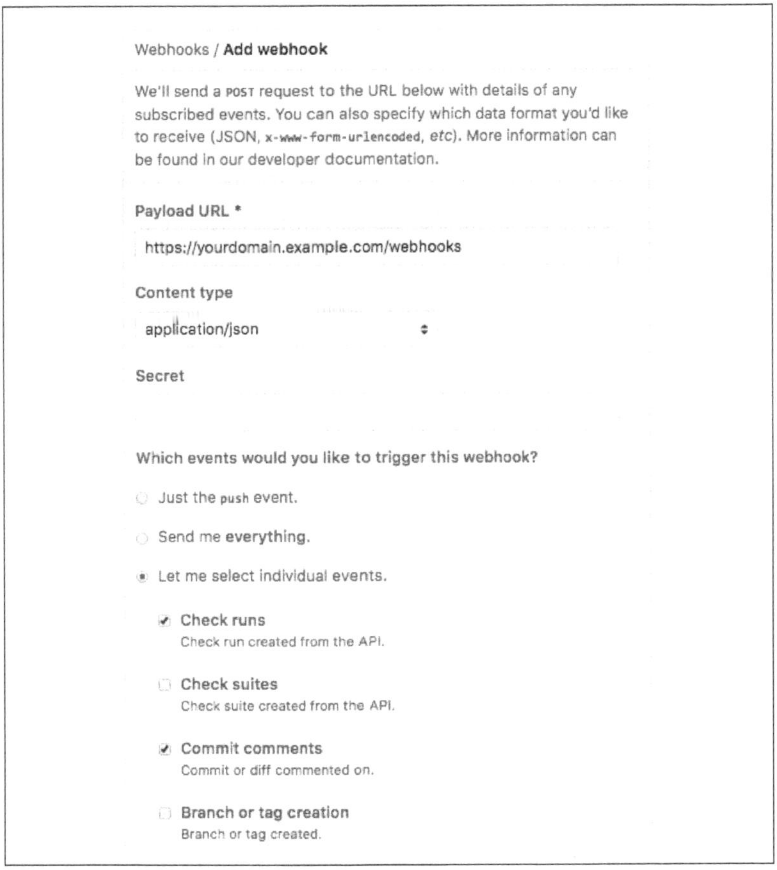

Figure 2-4. Configuring a GitHub WebHook

WebSockets

WebSocket (*https://en.wikipedia.org/wiki/WebSocket*) is a protocol used to establish a two-way streaming communication channel over a single Transport Control Protocol (TCP) connection. Although the protocol is generally used between a web client (e.g., a browser) and a server, it's sometimes used for server-to-server communication, as well.

The WebSocket protocol is supported by major browsers and often used by real-time applications. Slack uses WebSockets to send all kinds of events happening in a workspace to Slack's clients, including new messages, emoji reactions added to items, and channel creations. Slack also provides a WebSocket-based Real Time Messaging API (*https://api.slack.com/rtm*) to developers so that they can receive events from Slack in real time and send messages as users. Similarly, Trello (*https://blog.fogcreek.com/the-trello-tech-stack/*) uses WebSockets to push changes made by other people down from servers to browsers listening on the appropriate channels, and Blockchain (*https://blockchain.info/api/api_websocket*) uses its WebSocket API to send real-time notifications about new transactions and blocks.

WebSockets can enable full-duplex communication (server and client can communicate with each other simultaneously) at a low overhead. Additionally, they are designed to work over port 80 or 443, enabling them to work well with firewalls that might block other ports. This is an especially important consideration when it comes to enterprise developers. For example, some enterprise developers using Slack APIs prefer to use the WebSocket API over WebHooks because they are able to receive events from the Slack API securely without having to open up an HTTP WebHook endpoint to the internet where Slack can post messages.

WebSockets are great for fast, live streaming data and long-lived connections. However, be wary if you plan to make these available on mobile devices or in regions where connectivity can be spotty. Clients are supposed to keep the connection alive. If the connection dies, the client needs to reinitiate it. There are also issues related to scalability. Developers using Slack's WebSocket API must establish a connection for each team that uses their app (Figure 2-5). This means that if an app is installed on 10,000 Slack workspaces, the developer would be responsible for maintaining 10,000 connections between Slack servers and the app's server.

⬆ {"type":"tickle","id":16392}   28 18:12...
⬆ {"type":"typing","channel":"C0GEV71UG","id":16393}   50 18:12...
⬆ {"type":"message","channel":"C0GEV71UG","text":"new message","id":16394}   72 18:12...
⬇ {"ok":true,"reply_to":16394,"ts":"1519870324.000289","text":"new message"}   74 18:12...
⬆ {"type":"typing","channel":"C0GEV71UG","id":16395}   50 18:12...
⬆ {"type":"message","channel":"C0GEV71UG","text":"hi","id":16396}   63 18:12...
⬇ {"ok":true,"reply_to":16396,"ts":"1519870325.000226","text":"hi"}   65 18:12...
⬇ {"type":"channel_marked","channel":"C0GEV71UG","ts":"1519870325.000226","unread_count":0,"unread_count_disp...   231 18:12...
⬆ {"type":"typing","channel":"C0GEV71UG","id":16397}   50 18:12...
⬆ {"type":"message","channel":"C0GEV71UG","text":"Hey","id":16398}   64 18:12...
⬇ {"ok":true,"reply_to":16398,"ts":"1519870326.000314","text":"Hey"}   66 18:12...
⬆ {"type":"typing","channel":"C0GEV71UG","id":16399}   50 18:12...
⬆ {"type":"message","channel":"C0GEV71UG","text":"what's up","id":16400}   70 18:12...
⬇ {"ok":true,"reply_to":16400,"ts":"1519870328.000116","text":"what's up"}   72 18:12...
⬇ {"type":"channel_marked","channel":"C0GEV71UG","ts":"1519870328.000116","unread_count":0,"unread_count_disp...   231 18:12...
⬆ {"type":"ping","id":16401}   26 18:12...
⬇ {"type":"pong","reply_to":16401}   32 18:12...
⬇ {"type":"reaction_added","user":"U0H4TC2U8","item":{"type":"message","channel":"C0GEV71UG","ts":"1519870326....   227 18:12...
⬇ {"type":"pref_change","name":"emoji_use","value":"{\"train\":1,\"two\":3,\"one\":2,\"memo\":1,\"wave::skin-tone-3\":3,... 318 18:12...
⬇ {"type":"reaction_added","user":"U0H4TC2U8","item":{"type":"message","channel":"C0GEV71UG","ts":"1519870326....   227 18:12...

Figure 2-5. Frames sent over a full-duplex WebSocket connection between Slack and a browser

HTTP Streaming

With the HTTP request–response APIs, clients send an HTTP request and the server returns an HTTP response of a finite length (Figure 2-6). Now, it's possible to make the length of this response indefinite. With HTTP Streaming, the server can continue to push new data in a single long-lived connection opened by a client.

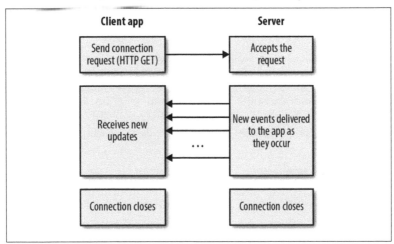

Figure 2-6. Client–server interaction with an HTTP Streaming API

To transmit data over a persistent connection from server to client, there are two options. The first option is for the server to set the

`Transfer-Encoding` header to chunked. This indicates to clients that data will be arriving in chunks of newline-delimited strings. For typical application developers, this is easy to parse.

Another option is to stream data via server-sent events (SSE). This option is great for clients consuming these events in a browser because they can use the standardized EventSource API.

Twitter (*https://developer.twitter.com/en/docs/tutorials/consuming-streaming-data*) utilizes the HTTP Streaming protocol to deliver data through a single connection opened between an app and Twitter's streaming API. The big benefit for developers is that they don't need to poll the Twitter API continuously for new tweets. Twitter's Streaming API can push new tweets over a single HTTP connection instead of a custom protocol. This saves resources for both Twitter and the developer.

HTTP Streaming is easy to consume. However, one of the issues with it is related to buffering. Clients and proxies often have buffer limits. They might not start rendering data to the application until a threshold is met. Also, if clients want to frequently change what kind of events they listen to, HTTP Streaming might not be ideal because it requires reconnections.

Table 2-3 summarizes the differences between the various event-driven API options.

Table 2-3. Comparison of event-driven APIs

	WebHooks	WebSockets	HTTP Streaming
What?	Event notification via HTTP callback	Two-way streaming connection over TCP	Long-lived connection over HTTP
Example services	Slack, Stripe, GitHub, Zapier, Google	Slack, Trello, Blockchain	Twitter, Facebook
Pros	• Easy server-to-server communication • Uses HTTP protocol	• Two-way streaming communication • Native browser support • Can bypass firewalls	• Can stream over simple HTTP • Native browser support • Can bypass firewalls

	WebHooks	WebSockets	HTTP Streaming
Cons	• Do not work across firewalls or in browsers • Handling failures, retries, security is hard	• Need to maintain a persistent connection • Not HTTP	• Bidirectional communication is difficult • Reconnections required to receive different events
When to use?	To trigger the server to serve real-time events	For two-way, real-time communication between browsers and servers	For one-way communication over simple HTTP

Closing Thoughts

There is no one-size-fits-all solution when it comes to selecting an API paradigm. Each of the API paradigms that we discussed in this chapter works well for certain kinds of use cases. You might need to support multiple paradigms, too. For example, the Slack API supports RPC-style APIs, WebSockets, and WebHooks. It's important for you to understand which solution will work best for your customers, which will help you meet your business goals, and what is possible with the constraints within which you are working.

In Chapter 3, we look into how you can secure your APIs. We cover how API providers are building authentication and authorization schemes. We also look extensively at OAuth, an open protocol used to secure authorization in a simple and standard way.

API Security

Security is a critical element of any web application, particularly so for APIs. New security issues and vulnerabilities are always being discovered, and it's important to protect your APIs from attacks. A security breach can be disastrous—poor security implementations can lead to loss of critical data as well as revenue.

To ensure an application is secure, there are many things engineers tend to do. This includes input validation, using the Secure Sockets Layer (SSL) protocol everywhere, validating content types, maintaining audit logs, and protecting against cross-site request forgery (CSRF) and cross-site scripting (XSS). All of these are important for any web application, and you should be doing them. Beyond these typical web application security practices, there are additional techniques that apply specifically to web APIs that you expose to developers outside your company. In this chapter, we look closely at those best practices and how companies are securing APIs in practice.

Authentication and Authorization

Authentication and authorization are two foundation elements of security:

Authentication
> The process of verifying who you are. Web applications usually accomplish this by asking you to log in with a username and password. This combination is checked against an existing valid username/password record to ensure the request is authentic.

Authorization

> The process of verifying that you are permitted to do what you are trying to do. For instance, a web application might allow you to view a page; however, it might not allow you to edit that page unless you are an administrator. That's authorization.

As you design an API, you need to think about how app developers will perform both authentication and authorization with your API. Early on, API providers started supporting Basic Authentication (*https://en.wikipedia.org/wiki/Basic_access_authentication*). It's the simplest technique used to enforce access control on the web. The clients send HTTP requests with an `Authorization` header which consists of the word "Basic" followed by a space and a string generated by combining username and password with a colon (*user name:password*) and encoding it with base64; for example:

```
Authorization: Basic dXNlcjpwYXNzd29yZA==
```

Although Basic Authentication is simple, it offers the least amount of security. If you use Basic Authentication for your API, to use a third-party developer's application, your users might need to share their username and password credentials with them. That has several disadvantages, including the following:

- Applications are required to store these credentials in clear text or in a way that they can decrypt them. If an application exposed the credentials via a bug or other means, that might leak private user data to a malicious hacker. Considering many people use the same password across multiple services, the data-loss impact on users could be pretty serious.

- Users cannot revoke access to a single application without revoking access to all the applications by changing the password.

- Applications get full access to user accounts. Users cannot limit access to selected resources.

For such reasons, Twitter decided to discontinue support for Basic Authentication for its core API in 2010.

OAuth

To address issues faced by Basic Authentication and other prevalent authentication and authorization mechanisms, OAuth (*https://*

oauth.net/) was introduced in 2007. OAuth is an open standard that allows users to grant access to applications without sharing passwords with them. The latest version of the standard, OAuth 2.0, is the industry-standard protocol for authorization. It has been adopted by several companies, including Amazon, Google, Facebook, GitHub, Stripe, and Slack.

The biggest benefit of OAuth is that users do not need to share passwords with applications. For example, say TripAdvisor wants to build an application that will use a user's Facebook identity, profile, friend list, and other Facebook data. With OAuth, TripAdvisor can redirect that user to Facebook, where they can authorize TripAdvisor to access their information, as demonstrated in Figure 3-1. After the user authorizes the sharing of data, TripAdvisor can then call the Facebook API to fetch this information.

Figure 3-1. The OAuth flow between TripAdvisor and Facebook

The second benefit of OAuth is that it allows API providers' users to grant selective permission. Each application has different requirements of what data it needs from an API provider. The OAuth framework allows API providers to grant access to one or more resources. For example, in the case of TripAdvisor in Figure 3-1, TripAdvisor would receive permission to read a user's profile, friends list, and more, but it cannot post on the user's behalf on Facebook.

Finally, if at some point a user would like to revoke TripAdvisor's access to their Facebook data, they can simply go to their Facebook settings and revoke it without changing their password.

Token Generation

With OAuth, applications use an access token to call APIs on behalf of a user. The generation of this token happens in a multistep flow. Before an application can start the OAuth flow, it needs to be registered with the API provider. During registration, developers provide a redirect URL—an application URL to which the API provider can redirect the authorizing user. The API provider issues a client ID and client secret that are unique to the application. The client ID can be public, whereas the client secret should be kept confidential.

After an application is registered, the application can generate an access token by following these steps:

1. The application directs the user to the API provider for authorization.

   Applications typically first show authorizing users a button labeled something like "Continue with Facebook." When users click the button, they are redirected to the API provider's authorization URL. While redirecting, the application sends the client ID, the permissions requested (i.e., access to the user's public profile or list of friends) in a parameter called scope, an optional unique string state parameter, and (optionally) a redirect URL.

2. The API provider seeks the user's authorization.

   As shown in Figure 3-2, the API provider should clearly indicate what permissions the application is requesting. If the user denies the authorization, they are redirected back to the application's redirect URL with an access_denied error. If the user approves the request, they are redirected back to the application with an authorization code.

Figure 3-2. Authorization screen presented by Slack to users

3. The application exchanges an authorization code for an access token.

   Upon successful authorization, applications can exchange the authorization code via an access token. The application will need to send the client ID, client secret, authorization code, and redirect URL to the API provider to receive an access token. The authorization code provided can be used only once; this helps in preventing replay attacks. Applications can then use this access token for accessing protected resources on behalf of the user.

Figure 3-3 depicts the OAuth 2.0 authorization flow used to issue access tokens to applications on behalf of users.

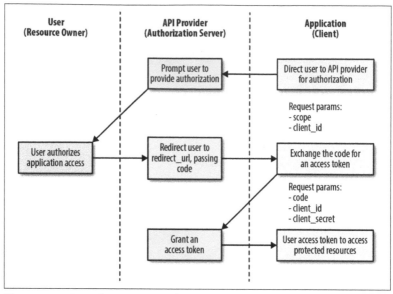

Figure 3-3. OAuth 2.0 access token grant flow

Scopes

OAuth scopes are used to limit an application's access to user data. For instance, an application might only need to identify a user. Rather than requesting access to all of the user's data, the application can request access to only the user's profile information by means of a granular OAuth scope. During authorization, the API provider will display all the requested scopes to the user. This way, users will know what permissions they are granting to an application.

Defining scopes for an API is an interesting problem. Many APIs offer simple read, write, and combo read/write scopes. For instance, the Twitter API offers three levels of permissions via scopes:

- Read only
- Read and write
- Read, write, and access direct messages

Often, API providers open up their APIs without thinking too much about scopes. Only when the API begins to be widely adopted or is being abused do they start realizing the need for additional scopes. At that time, introducing new scopes becomes complicated. It's important to think about your goals and use cases before you decide which scopes you might want to support. Granular scopes help in ensuring that applications have only the permissions they need. At the same time, too many scopes can create confusion for users and developers.

Beyond typical read/write scopes, here are some additional considerations for defining your scopes:

A minimal scope
You may want to offer a scope that that provides only basic user information, like a name and profile picture (and nothing else). Applications building sign-in flows can use this to identify a user. Most API providers, like Slack, Facebook, and Heroku, offer such a scope.

Isolate scopes for protecting sensitive information
It's important to protect sensitive information on your service with a separate scope. When an application requests this sensitive scope, users should be shown a clear warning indicating what is being shared with the application. Heroku introduced "read-protected" and "write-protected" scopes to manage access to resources, like an app's configuration variables, which contain secrets like database connection strings.

Similarly, GitHub introduced a different scope to read information about private repositories. Twitter also added a scope that would grant access to direct messages when it realized many apps were abusing the read scope by accessing them even when they didn't need to.

Differentiate scopes for different kinds of resources
Many large API providers that have multiple types of services and features choose to split scopes by functionality. For example, the Slack API has different scopes for reading and writing messages, pins, stars, reactions, channels, users, and other resources. Similarly, GitHub has different scopes for accessing different resources, like the repositories, managing organization, public keys, notifications, and gists. This means that an application requesting access to only a user's repositories will not be granted access to that user's gists.

Lessons Learned from Slack's Move to Granular OAuth Scopes

When Slack launched its OAuth system support, the scopes available to developers were broad. For instance, authorizing an application for the read scope meant that the app would gain read access to all of the user's messages, channels, reactions, stars, files, and other resources. This went far beyond what was generally needed by most apps in practice.

In late 2015, Slack introduced 27 granular OAuth scopes (*https:// medium.com/slack-developer-blog/new-and-improved-oauth-scopes-4894b2cc159d*). For each type of resource in Slack, like channels, groups, files, reactions, and stars, read and write scopes were added. This way, applications could specifically request the scopes that they needed. The big benefit of the new granular scopes was that the apps received only the permissions essential to perform their intended function. Moreover, users felt more comfortable with giving applications access to limited resources, which improved the conversion rate for application installations.

Token and Scope Validation

After developers have received an access token, they can begin making API requests using this access by setting the HTTP `Authorization` header, as shown in Example 3-1.

Example 3-1. Request to Slack API with access token

```
POST /api/chat.postMessage
HOST slack.com
Content-Type: application/json
Authorization: Bearer xoxp-16501860-a24afg234
{
 "channel":"C0GEV71UG",
 "text":"This a message text",
 "attachments":[{"text":"attachment text"}]
 }
```

When receiving these requests, there are two things that API providers' servers need to verify. The first is that the access token is valid. You need to match the given access token with the granted access tokens in your database. The second is that the access token has the required scope for the action that the request is supposed to perform. If either check fails, the server should return an error.

Apart from errors, it's also useful to return more metadata about which scopes were needed and which scopes were provided. Many APIs, like those for GitHub and Slack, return these two headers:

- X-OAuth-Scopes lists the scopes for which a token has been authorized.

- X-Accepted-OAuth-Scopes lists the scopes that the action requires.

Example 3-2 presents sample OAuth headers returned by the Git-Hub API.

Example 3-2. OAuth scope headers in the GitHub API response

```
curl -H "Authorization: token OAUTH-TOKEN"\
  https://api.github.com/users/saurabhsahni -I
HTTP/1.1 200 OK
X-OAuth-Scopes: repo, user
X-Accepted-OAuth-Scopes: user
```

In case a token is missing the required scope, to make troubleshooting easier for developers, it's useful to return more verbose errors indicating the provided scope along with the scope that the action requires. For example, as shown in Example 3-3, the Slack API returns such verbose errors.

Example 3-3. Response from the Slack API when a valid token is missing the required scope

```
{
    "ok": false,
    "error": "missing_scope",
    "needed": "chat:write:user",
    "provided": "identify,bot,users:read",
}
```

Token Expiry and Refresh Tokens

The OAuth protocol allows limiting the validity of the access token issued in the OAuth flow. Many APIs choose to issue tokens that expire in a few hours or days. This way, if a token is compromised, the impact can be contained. If you issue access tokens with limited validity, you need to provide a way for applications to obtain a new token, typically without intervention from the end user. One way to do this is by issuing *refresh tokens*.

A refresh token is a special type of token used to obtain a new access token when the current access token expires. Applications need to provide the client ID, client secret, and refresh token to generate a new access token. Refresh tokens are a standard way of renewing expired access tokens. API providers, like Google, Salesforce, Asana, Stripe, and Amazon, support refresh tokens.

Even if your access tokens do not expire, it can be a good idea to share refresh tokens. This way, in case of a compromise, an app developer can rotate an existing access token and generate a new one. This is why the Stripe API supports refresh tokens, even though the access tokens it grants do not expire.

Short-lived access tokens are more secure for the following reasons:

- If an access token is compromised, it will work only until it expires.
- If a refresh token is compromised, it will be useless without the client secret, which is typically not stored along with access tokens and refresh tokens.
- If both the refresh token and the client secret are compromised and the attacker generates a new access token, the compromise can potentially be detected because typically refresh tokens are one-time use only and only one party can use the API (per refresh token) at a time.

Storytime: Slack's Long-Lived Tokens

Slack's main product is communication software for teams. Part of its product offering is an API that enables third-party developers to create apps and bots within Slack.

The appetite for third-party developers building on Slack's API was demonstrated long before Slack released its OAuth support. As a result, many developers found ways to "hack" their apps by creating API tokens through various mechanisms and embedding them directly in their application code. Some developers weren't careful and published these tokens on their GitHub pages. This was a problem because Slack's tokens were long-lived and would effectively never expire.

In an effort to ensure that Slack users were able to maintain their privacy and to prevent unintended usage of these tokens, Slack created a scraper that would search GitHub's open source code repositories for instances of Slack tokens. Any tokens that were found were automatically revoked and the developer was notified.

Short-lived tokens mitigate the risk of abuse due to such leaks. In May 2018, Slack announced that it is working on introducing short-lived access tokens.

Listing and Revoking Authorizations

For various reasons, a user might want to know which applications can access their data and might want to revoke access to one or more of them. To support this use case, most API providers typically offer a page that lists the applications that a user has authorized along with the ability to revoke access, as illustrated in Figure 3-4.

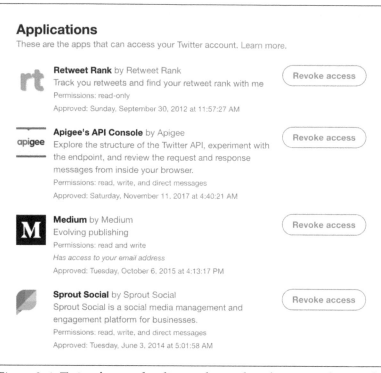

Applications

These are the apps that can access your Twitter account. Learn more.

Retweet Rank by Retweet Rank
Track you retweets and find your retweet rank with me
Permissions: read-only
Approved: Sunday, September 30, 2012 at 11:57:27 AM

Revoke access

Apigee's API Console by Apigee
Explore the structure of the Twitter API, experiment with
the endpoint, and review the request and response
messages from inside your browser.
Permissions: read, write, and direct messages
Approved: Saturday, November 11, 2017 at 4:40:21 AM

Revoke access

Medium by Medium
Evolving publishing
Permissions: read and write
Has access to your email address
Approved: Tuesday, October 6, 2015 at 4:13:17 PM

Revoke access

Sprout Social by Sprout Social
Sprout Social is a social media management and
engagement platform for businesses.
Permissions: read, write, and direct messages
Approved: Tuesday, June 3, 2014 at 5:01:58 AM

Revoke access

Figure 3-4. Twitter's page that lists authorized applications, along with a "Revoke access" button for each

As well as providing the ability to revoke authorizations in the UI, it's a good idea to provide APIs that give users the ability to revoke access tokens and refresh tokens. This way, a developer who wants to revoke a token, due to a compromise or for other reasons, can do so programmatically.

OAuth Best Practices

Here's a list of best practices that you might like to consider when building your own authorization server using OAuth:

state *parameter support*

The state parameter is an optional authentication parameter that you use to help mitigate CSRF attacks. API providers implementing OAuth should support this parameter. The state parameter is a string generated by the developer for authenticating the user and is passed to the authorization endpoint. The

API provider then passes this string back to the redirect URL along with the authorization code in exchange for the access token.

Short-lived authorization codes

Generated authorization codes should expire within a few minutes and should be one-time use only. This way, an attacker cannot use them to generate tokens along with the authorized application.

One-time-use refresh tokens

If you are building an application that stores very sensitive data, consider restricting your refresh tokens to one-time use only. You can issue a new one when an access token is renewed. Although single-use refresh tokens add complexity for developers, they do help in detecting compromises of refresh tokens and client secrets. That said, it is a good idea to allow applications to use refresh tokens for a small window of time so that they can retry if there was a network failure or another issue. The Fitbit API allows a refresh token to be reused for up to two minutes.

Ability to reset the client secret

You should provide developers with the ability to reset the client secret. This way, if client secrets and refresh tokens are compromised, applications can stop an attacker with a leaked client secret from renewing access tokens.

OAuth scopes for sensitive information

Protect sensitive information on your service by using dedicated OAuth scopes. This way, your users will not grant access to sensitive information to every application that might not need it.

HTTPS endpoints

Because access tokens are sent as part of every HTTP request, it's important that your API endpoints require HTTPS. This prevents man-in-the-middle attacks.

Verify redirect URL

When the optional redirect URL is provided, during an authorization request, ensure that it matches to one of the registered URLs for the application. If not, the API server must show an error without showing the authorization prompt. This ensures that any returned secrets are not exposed to an attacker.

Disallow rendering the authorization screen in iframes

Use the X-Frame-Options header to deny rendering an authorization page in an iframe. This prevents clickjacking attacks, where a malicious site tricks a user into clicking an element that seems harmless but actually leads to clicking a button like "Authorize" on another site.

Keep users informed

You should notify users over a medium like email when a new authorization is granted. This way, users can be alerted if the authorization was unintended.

Prohibit misleading application names

Do not allow apps to use names that might mislead users into thinking that an outside application was created by your company. One way to enforce this is by denying apps permission to use your company name in OAuth application names. In 2017, an attacker created a Google OAuth application with the name "Google Docs" along with the Google Docs logo, as depicted in Figure 3-5. A million Google accounts were successfully phished (*http://www.bbc.com/news/technology-39845545*) by this application.

Figure 3-5. A malicious non-Google app named "Google Docs" phished one million Google accounts in 2017

Lessons Learned from Facebook: A Balancing Act

From 2016 to 2018, Facebook's policies came under intense scrutiny for creating addictive usage patterns while enabling targeted advertising. This is exactly what the platform was intended to do. At the same time, developers were able to intensively mine customer data, in accordance with the API's permissions and customer access grants, but in violation of Facebook's terms of service (ToS). Here are some takeaways from the incident:

- Ensure that your customers know what they're agreeing to. In the OAuth flow, make sure it's clear exactly what permission the customer is granting. As a bonus, enable customers to grant fewer and more granular scopes, potentially adding some as their usage patterns change. However, this is a balancing act, because if the scopes are too granular, customers might not read them. Make the strings readable and understandable.

- Ensure that you monitor third-party developers' applications and actively search for potential ToS violations. You might want to turn these apps off or rate-limit them so that they're not able to continue the behavior.

Yes, the customer has authorized the data access. But the trust is between you and the customer, not between the customer and the third-party application. At the end of the day, you have a higher stake in how your platform is perceived by your customers.

As of this writing, consumers don't always understand the difference between privacy and security. This is better for enterprise customers. If you're building a consumer product, you need to think hard about how you're communicating the capabilities of your platform to your end users.

WebHooks Security

As discussed in Chapter 2, a WebHook is simply a URL where API providers send a POST request when something happens. For instance, Stripe sends notifications about new payments to Web-Hook URLs. Similarly, whenever you open a Pull Request in Git-Hub, GitHub sends a POST request to the developer's configured WebHook URL(s).

Securing WebHooks is slightly different from securing web APIs. Because the WebHook URLs are generally publicly accessible on the internet, it's important for the developers to be able to ensure the POST request actually came from the stated sender. In the absence of such a verification, an attacker can forge a request to the WebHook URL. Although there are no standards like OAuth that are used to secure WebHooks, there are some common patterns that API providers follow.

Verification Tokens

A *verification token* is a secret shared between applications and API providers. As shown in Figure 3-6, API providers like Slack issue a unique verification token to every application. With each dispatched WebHook request, Slack sends a verification token. Applications match the token received as part of the request with the recorded value. If they do not match, the application ignores the request. This way, applications can verify that a request actually came from Slack.

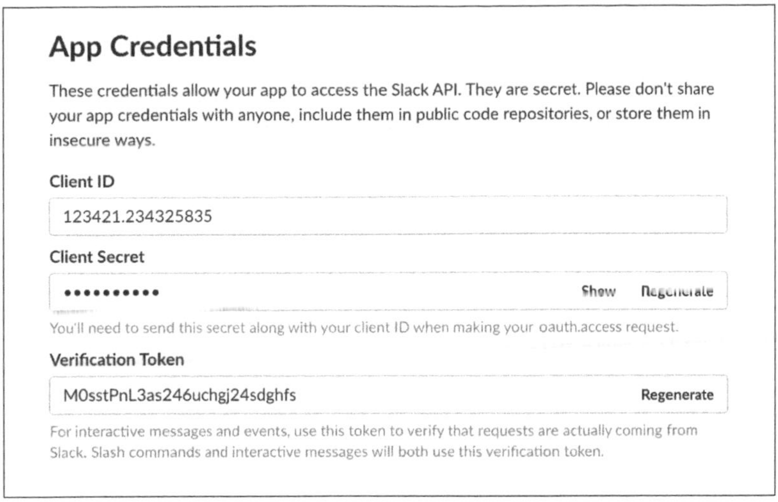

App Credentials

These credentials allow your app to access the Slack API. They are secret. Please don't share your app credentials with anyone, include them in public code repositories, or store them in insecure ways.

Client ID

```
123421.234325835
```

Client Secret

•••••••••   Show   Regenerate

You'll need to send this secret along with your client ID when making your oauth.access request.

Verification Token

```
MOsstPnL3as246uchgj24sdghfs                            Regenerate
```

For interactive messages and events, use this token to verify that requests are actually coming from Slack. Slash commands and interactive messages will both use this verification token.

Figure 3-6. Credentials of a Slack app, including verification token

Verification tokens are simple to implement, from both the API provider's and the developer's perspective. A simple comparison check can ensure the request came from the desired sender. However, verification tokens also offer limited security because they are sent in plain text with every request. If a verification token is leaked or compromised, an attacker can forge WebHook requests.

Request Signing and WebHook Signatures

Signatures are among the most common ways API providers choose to secure WebHooks. WebHook payloads are typically signed by computing a hash-based message authentication code (HMAC) of a shared secret plus the request body, and the signature is sent as part of a request header. Applications then verify the authenticity of the request by computing the same HMAC and comparing it to the value set in the header. API providers, like Stripe and GitHub, use this mechanism to secure WebHooks.

Preventing replay attacks

A replay attack is a form of attack in which an attacker retransmits a WebHook with a valid signature. To mitigate such attacks (as shown in the t=1492774577 part of Example 3-4), API providers like Stripe include a request timestamp in the message payload. If the timestamp is too old, applications can reject the request.

Example 3-4. A signature header from a Stripe WebHook request

```
Stripe-Signature: t=1492774577,
    v1=5257a869e7ecebeda32affa62cdca3fa51cad7e77a0e56ff536d0c,
    v0=6ffbb59b2300aae63f272406069a9788598b792a944a07aba816ed
```

Mutual Transport Layer Security

When you connect to an *https://* URL with the Transport Layer Security (TLS) Handshake Protocol, the server sends its certificate to the client. The client then verifies the server's certificate before trusting the response.

With *mutual TLS*, the server and client both authenticate each other. The server sends the client a certificate request. The client (WebHook provider, in this case) then responds with a certificate. The server verifies the client's certificate before trusting the request.

Although request signing is implemented within application logic, you can implement Mutual TLS at a lower level. This way, developers can enforce high security while opening a firewall for an API without requiring anything of the application developers. This is especially useful for enterprise developers.

Mutual TLS is typically used in business-to-business applications. API providers like DocuSign support Mutual TLS.

Thin Payloads and API Retrieval

One of the fundamental problems with WebHook signatures and verification tokens is that both of these methods rely on developers to do the right thing. They do not enforce authentication. Different application developers can follow different security standards, and it's difficult to determine whether they are verifying WebHook requests.

A more secure option is to send limited information in the payload indicating to the application that something has changed. To retrieve the full event, the application would need to make a subsequent request to the web API. The key benefit of this approach is that even if applications do not verify the WebHook, they will receive the full event only after making regular authenticated requests to a web API.

Google uses this method for securing WebHooks. Gmail's API allows applications to subscribe to watch for changes in an inbox using WebHooks. When something changes, Gmail sends a WebHook request, including the email address and an ID for the change (base64-encoded in the `data` field, as shown in Example 3-5). Applications can call Gmail's `history.list` web API to retrieve the full change details.

Example 3-5. Gmail's thin WebHook message payload

```
{
  message:
  {
    data: "eyJlbWFpbEFkZHJlc3MiOiAidXNlckBleGFtcGxlLmNvbSIsICJoaXN0b
    message_id: "1234567890",
  }
  subscription: "mysubscription"
}
```

WebHook Security Best Practices

Enforcing security standards on WebHooks is complicated. Here are some security best practices that you should keep in mind when building support for WebHooks:

- Avoid sending sensitive information as part of WebHooks. Never send passwords or secrets as part of the WebHook payloads. Use authenticated API requests to send any sensitive information.

- If you are signing WebHooks, include a timestamp in the payload. This way, applications can implement checks for replay attacks.

- Support regeneration of shared secrets (used as a verification token or one for signing the WebHook). In case of a compromised secret, an application developer can rotate this secret and ensure authenticity of future requests.

- Provide developers with SDKs and sample code that verify the authenticity of WebHook requests and reject invalid requests.

Closing Thoughts

Security is difficult. Securing APIs is even more difficult. Once you have applications using a security mechanism, it is hard to change it, and a vulnerability may require many developers to patch applications that are using the API. So it's important to think deeply about security implications before you release your API. Although innovating new security mechanisms and inventing your own can be enticing, it could be a big mistake. Unless you have security experts designing and vetting your new security mechanism, it's hard to ensure that it's free from vulnerabilities. If you rely on a well-designed, tested, and open security standard that has been examined and tested by hackers and experts over the years, your chances of running into a major security vulnerability will be far lower.

In Chapter 4, we cover various tactical best practices for designing your API that can help you to deliver a great developer experience.

Design Best Practices

In the previous chapters, we gave an overview of various approaches for transmitting data via your web API. Now that you're familiar with the landscape of transport and have an understanding of how to choose between various patterns and frameworks, we want to provide some tactical best practices to help your developers get the most out of your API.

Designing for Real-Life Use Cases

When designing an API, it's best to make decisions that are grounded in specific, real-life use cases. Let's dig into this idea a bit more. Think about the developers who are using your API. What tasks should they be able to complete with your API? What types of apps should developers be able to build? For some companies, this is as targeted as "developers should be able to charge customer credit cards." For other companies, the answer can be more open-ended: "developers should be able to create a full suite of interactive consumer-quality applications."

After you have your use cases defined, make sure that developers can actually do the things you want them to do using your API.

Quite often APIs are designed based on the internal architecture of the application, leaking details of the implementation. This leads to confusion for third-party developers and a bad developer experience. That's why it's so important to focus not on exposing on your company's internal infrastructure but on the experience that an outside developer should have when interacting with your API. For a concrete example of how to define key use cases, see the section "Outline Key Use Cases" in Chapter 5.

When you get started with a design, it's easy to imagine many "what-ifs" before implementation and testing. Although these questions are useful during the brainstorming phase, they can lead a design astray by tempting you to try and solve too many problems at once. By picking a specific workflow or use case, you will be able to focus on one design and then test whether it works for your users.

Expert Advice

When we asked Ido Green, developer advocate at Google, what makes an API good, his top answer was *focus*:

> "The API should enable developers to do one thing really well. It's not as easy as it sounds, and you want to be clear on what the API is not going to do as well."

 If you need help narrowing down the developer audience to a specific one, see Chapter 8.

Designing for a Great Developer Experience

Like we spend time thinking about the user experience delivered via a user interface, it's important to think about the developer experience delivered via an API. Developers have a low bar for abandoning APIs, so bad experiences result in attrition. By the same token, usability is the bare minimum for keeping a developer using your API. Good experiences get love from developers: they will in turn, become the most creative innovators using your API as well as evangelists for your API.

Make It Fast and Easy to Get Started

It's important for developers to be able to understand your API and to get up and running quickly. Developers may be using your API to avoid having to build out a secondary product suite to support their main product. Don't make them regret that decision with an API that's opaque and difficult to use.

Documentation can go a long way toward helping developers get started. In addition to documents that outline the specifications of an API, it can be helpful to have tutorials or Getting Started guides. A tutorial is an interactive interface to teach developers about your API. You might have developers answer questions or fill in "code" in an input area. A guide is a more contextual document than a specification. It provides information for developers at a certain point in time—typically when getting started, but sometimes when updating or converting from one version or feature to another.

In some cases, you can supplement the ease of use by providing interactive documentation online, where developers have a sandbox to test out your API. For more on sandboxes, see Chapter 9. Oftentimes, developers can use these interfaces to test code and preview results without having to implement authentication. Figure 4-1 presents an example of Stripe's UI for this.

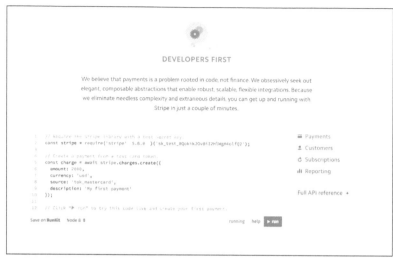

Figure 4-1. Developers can try the Stripe API without signing up

In addition to interactive documentation, tools such as software development kits (SDKs) can go a long way toward helping developers use your API. These code packages are designed to help developers get up and running quickly with their projects by simplifying some of the transactional layers and setup of an application.

For an ideal experience, developers should be able to try out your APIs without logging in or signing up. If you cannot avoid that, you should provide a simple signup or application creation flow that captures the minimum required information. If your API is protected by OAuth, you should provide a way for developers to generate access tokens in the UI. Implementing OAuth is cumbersome for developers, and in the absence of easy ways to generate these tokens, you will see a significant drop-off rate at this point.

Work Toward Consistency

You want your API to be intuitively consistent. That should be reflected in your endpoint names, input parameters, and output responses. Developers should be able to guess parts of your API even without reading the documentation. Unless you are making a significant version bump or large release, it's best to work toward consistency when designing new aspects of an existing API.

For example, you might have previously named a group of resources "users" and named your API endpoints accordingly, but you now realize that it makes more sense to call them "members." It can be very tempting to work toward the "correctness" of the new world rather than focus on consistency with the old. But if the objects are the same, it could be very confusing to developers to sometimes refer to them as "users" and other times as "members" in URI components, request parameters, and elsewhere. For the majority of incremental changes, consistency with the existing design patterns will work best for your users.

As another example, if in some places you have a response field called user and sometimes its type is an integer ID but sometimes its type is an object, each and every developer receiving those two response payloads needs to check whether user is an int ID or an object. This logic leads to code bloat in developers' code bases, which is a suboptimal experience.

This can show up in your own code as well. If you have SDKs that you're maintaining, you will need to add more and more logic to handle these inconsistencies and to make a seamless interface for developers. You might as well do this at the API level by maintaining consistency instead of introducing new names for the same things.

Consistency generally means that there are a number of patterns and conventions repeated throughout your API, in such a way that developers can begin to predict how to use your API without seeing the documentation. That could include anything from data access patterns to error handling to naming. The reason consistency is important is that it reduces the cognitive load on developers who are trying to figure out your API. Consistency helps your existing developers in adapting new features by reducing forks in their code, and it helps new developers hit the ground running with everything you've built on your API. In contrast, with less consistency, different developers will need to reimplement the same logic over and over again.

 For more on this topic, skip ahead to Chapter 5.

Make Troubleshooting Easy

Another best practice for designing APIs is making troubleshooting easy for developers. This can be done through returning meaningful errors as well as by building tooling.

Meaningful errors

What's in an error? An error can occur in many places along your code path, from an authorization error during an API request, to a business logic error when a particular entity doesn't exist, to a lower-level database connection error. When designing an API, it is helpful to make troubleshooting as easy as possible by systematically organizing and categorizing errors and how they are returned. Incorrect or unclear errors are frustrating and can negatively affect adoption of your APIs. Developers can get stuck and just give up.

Meaningful errors are easy to understand, unambiguous, and actionable. They help developers to understand the problem and to address it. Providing these errors with details leads to a better developer experience. Error codes that are *machine-readable* strings allow developers to programmatically handle errors in their code bases.

In addition to these strings, it is useful to add longer-form errors, either in the documentation or somewhere else in the payload. These are sometimes referred to as *human-readable* errors. Even better, personalize these errors per developer. For instance, with the Stripe API, when you use a test key in your live mode, it returns an error such as:

```
No such token tok_test_60neARX2. A similar object exists in
test mode, but a live mode key was used to make this request.
```

Table 4-1 shows example errors (both recommended and not) for certain situations.

Table 4-1. Example error codes for different situations

Situation	Recommended	Not recommended
Authentication failed because token is revoked	`token_revoked`	`invalid_auth`
Value passed for name exceeded max length	`name_too_long`	`invalid_name`
Credit card has expired	`expired_card`	`invalid_card`
Cannot refund because a charge has already been refunded	`charge_already_refunded`	`cannot_refund`

To begin designing your system of errors, you might map out your backend architecture along the code path of an API request. The goal of this is not to expose your backend architecture but to categorize the errors that happen and to identify which ones to expose to developers. From the moment an API request is made, what are the critical actions that are taken to fulfill the request? Map out the various high-level categories of errors that occur during the course of an API request, from the beginning of the request to any service boundaries within your architecture. Table 4-2 provides a brief example to get you started.

Table 4-2. Group errors into high-level categories

Error category	Examples
System-level error	Database connection issue
	Backend service connection issue
	Fatal error
Business logic error	Rate-limited
	Request fulfilled, but no results were found
	Business-related reason to deny access to information
API request formatting error	Required request parameters are missing
	Combined request parameters are invalid together
Authorization error	OAuth credentials are invalid for request
	Token has expired

After grouping your error categories throughout your code path, think about what level of communication is meaningful for these errors. Some options include HTTP status codes and headers, as well as machine-readable "codes" or more verbose human-readable error messages returned in the response payload. Keep in mind that you'll want to return an error response in a format consistent with your non-error responses. For example, if you return a JSON response on a successful request, you should ensure that the error is returned in the same format.

You might also want a mechanism to bubble up errors from a service boundary to a consistent format from your API output. For example, a service you depend on might have a variety of connection errors. You would let the developer know that something went wrong and that they should try again.

In most cases, you want to be as specific as possible to help your developers take the correct next course of action. Other times, however, you might want to occlude the original issue by returning something more generic. This might be for security reasons. For example, you probably don't want to bubble up your database errors to the outside world and reveal too much information about your database connections.

Table 4-3 offers examples of how you might begin to organize your errors as you design your API.

Table 4-3. Organize your errors into status codes, headers, machine-readable codes, and human-readable strings

Error category	HTTP status	HTTP headers	Error code (machine-readable)	Error message (human-readable)
System-level error	500	--	--	--
Business logic error	429	Retry-After	`rate_limit_exceeded`	"You have been rate-limited. See Retry-After and try again."
API request formatting error	400	--	`missing_required_parameter`	"Your request was missing a {user} parameter."
Auth error	401	--	`invalid_request`	"Your ClientId is invalid."

As you begin to organize your errors, you might recognize patterns around which you can create some automatic messaging. For example, you might define the schema for your API to require specific parameters and to have a library that automatically checks for these at the beginning of the request. This same library could format the verbose error in the response payload.

You'll want to create a way to document these errors publicly on the web. You can build this into your API description language (see Chapter 7) or documentation mechanism. Think about the various layers of errors before writing the documents, because it can become complicated to describe multiple factors if there are many different types of errors. You might also want to consider using verbose response payloads to link to your public documentation. This is where you'll give developers more information on the error they received as well as how to recover from it.

For even more structured and detailed recommendations on meaningful errors and problem details for HTTP APIs, see RFC 7807
(*https://tools.ietf.org/html/rfc7807*).

Build tooling

In addition to making troubleshooting easy for developers, you
should make it easy for yourself by building internal and external
tools.

Logging on HTTP statuses, errors and their frequencies, and other
request metadata is valuable to have, for both internal and external
use, when it comes to troubleshooting developer issues. Figure 4-2
shows Stripe's dashboard with detailed logs that make it convenient
for developers to troubleshoot. There are many off-the-shelf logging
solutions available. However, when implementing one, before you
troubleshoot real-time traffic, be sure to respect customer privacy by
redacting any personally identifiable information (PII). For more on
developer tools that help developers debug and troubleshoot, see
Chapter 9.

Figure 4-2. The Stripe API dashboard with request logs

Besides logging, when building an API, it's helpful to create dashboards to help developers analyze aggregate metadata on API requests. For example, you could use an analytics platform to rank the most-used API endpoints, identify unused API parameters, triage common errors, and define success metrics.

Like for logging, many analytics platforms are available off the shelf. You can present the information in high-level dashboards that provide a visual display in a time-based manner. For example, you might want to show the number of errors per hour over the past week. Additionally, you might want to provide developers complete request logs with details about the original request, whether it succeeded or failed, and the response returned.

Make Your API Extensible

No matter how well you've designed your API, there will always be a need for change and growth as your product evolves and developer adoption increases. This means that you need to make your API extensible by creating a strategy for evolving it. This enables you as the API provider and your developer ecosystem to innovate. Additionally, it can provide a mechanism to deal with breaking changes. Let's dive into the idea of extensibility and explore how to incorporate early feedback, versioning an API, and maintaining backward compatibility. For more details on scaling APIs by developing your API design, see Chapter 6.

Expert Advice

APIs should provide primitives that can enable new workflows and not simply mirror the workflows of your application. The creation of an API acts as a gate for what the API's users can do. If you provide too low-level access, you could end up with a confusing integration experience and you push too much work on the integrators. If you provide too high-level access, you could end up with most integrations simply mirroring what your own application does. You need to find the right balance to enable workflows you hadn't considered either as part of your application or within the API itself in order to enable innovation. Consider what your own engineers would want in an API to build the next interesting feature for your application and then make that a part of your public API.

—Kyle Daigle, director of ecosystem engineering at GitHub

One aspect of extensibility is ensuring that you have created an opportunity for feedback with your top partners (for more on top partners, read Chapter 10). You need a way to release certain features or fields and to give certain privileged developers the option to test these changes without releasing the changes to the public. Some would call this a "beta" or "early adopter" program. For more on these programs, see Chapter 10. This feedback is extremely valuable in helping you decide whether your API has been designed in a way that achieves its goals. It gives you a chance to make changes before adoption has become prevalent and before significant changes require a lot of communication or operational overhead.

In some cases, you might want to version your API. Building a versioning system is easier if it's baked into the design at an early stage. The longer you wait to implement versioning, the more complicated it becomes to execute. That's because it becomes more and more difficult as time goes on to update your code base's dependency patterns so that old versions maintain backward compatibility. The benefit of versioning is that it allows you to make breaking changes with new versions while maintaining backward compatibility for old versions. A breaking change is a change that, when made, would stop an existing app from continuing to function as it was functioning before using your APIs.

For more on API versioning, see "Outline Key User Stories" on page 64.

Storytime: Slack's Translation Layer

In 2017 Slack launched its Enterprise Grid product, which was a federated model of its previous offering. As a result of this federation, Slack had to fundamentally change its user data model so that users could belong to multiple "workspaces."

In the API, users previously had only a single ID. However, in the new federated model, each user had a main (global) user ID for the Enterprise Grid and a local user ID for each workspace. When existing teams migrated to the Enterprise Grid product, their user IDs were slated to change. This would have broken any third-party apps relying on a fixed user ID in the API.

When Slack's engineering team realized this problem, it went back to the drawing board to figure out what could be done to maintain backward compatibility for third-party developers. That's when the team decided to create a translation layer. This additional infra-structure would silently translate user IDs to be consistent with the ones that developers had previously received.

Although the decision to build this translation layer delayed the Enterprise Grid product launch by several months, it was mission-critical for Slack to ensure that its API remained backward compat-ible.

For companies and products that businesses rely on, maintaining backward-compatible versions is a difficult requirement. That's especially true for apps that don't experience a high rate of change. For a lot of enterprise software, there isn't somebody dedicated to updating versions, and there's no incentive for a company to invest in updating versions just because you've released a new one. Many internet-connected hardware products also use APIs, but hardware does not always have a mechanism to update its software. Plus, hardware can be around for a long time—think about how long you owned your last TV or router. For those reasons, it is sometimes imperative that you maintain backward compatibility with previous API versions.

That said, maintaining versions does have a cost. If you don't have the capacity to support old versions for years, or if you anticipate very few changes to your API, by all means skip the versions and adopt an additive change strategy that also maintains backward compatibility in a single, stable version.

If you anticipate major breaking changes and updates *at any time in your future*, we strongly recommend setting up a versioning system. Even if it takes years to get to your first major version change, at least you've got the system ready to go. The overhead of creating a system of version management at the beginning is much lower than that of adding it in later, when it's urgently needed.

For more on API versioning, see Chapter 7.

Storytime: Deprecating an API at Twitch

In 2018, online video streaming platform Twitch decided to deprecate an API and provide a new API. After it announced the old API's deprecation and end of life (shutdown), Twitch received a lot of feedback from developers who said that they needed more time to handle the breaking change or their integrations would be broken. Because of that feedback, Twitch decided to extend the end of life of the old API to give developers ample time to move their code to the new one.

Closing Thoughts

Meeting the needs of your users is at the core of solid API design. In this chapter, we covered a number of best practices to help you achieve a great developer experience.

As you build your API and developer ecosystem, you might discover more best practices specific to your company, your product, and your users.

In Chapter 5, we put these ideas into practice and walk you through the practical steps for using everything you've learned in this book thus far to design an API.

Design in Practice

Now that we've provided guidance on API paradigms, security, and best practices, it's time for a hands-on, practical exercise in designing APIs. In this chapter, we take everything we covered in the first part of the book and use a fictitious example to explore different considerations.

In addition, we provide insights into how to create an effective design process so that you'll be able to design APIs on your own for whatever your use case may be.

Throughout this section, we focus heavily on the user experience to anchor our design decisions. Today's consumers are accustomed to excellent product experiences that suit their needs and lifestyle, not just products that get the job done. This high expectation for quality of experience goes beyond the products that people purchase. It extends to the apps that they use and the developer experience they expect when using APIs.

We might be building businesses and companies, but we don't design APIs for ourselves. We design APIs for the systems *receiving* the data and, more importantly, for the people who build those systems. If those developers cannot use the data we've provided, we have ultimately failed to create a useful design.

In the following sections, we use two different scenarios to explore how to begin with a user-centric design process and how to get feedback along the way. There are many methodologies to design, and the following process is simply a framework from which to start.

The most important aspect of this particular methodology is that it is designed to solicit feedback in a way that will result in decisions that ultimately benefit the API user.

If you'd like to follow along with your own example, you might want to use the Appendix A.

Scenario 1

To get us started with a practical example, here's a simple, fictitious scenario that we will use for the first part of this chapter:

> You are the lead engineer in a fast-growing image archive startup called MyFiles. The company's main product allows individual users and companies to privately archive data. Now that there is a steady stream of new users and lots of archival metadata, you and the team think there is a big potential in creating and publishing an API. As the lead engineer, you've been tasked with launching the new API within the next quarter.

Define Business Objectives

Before you begin coding or writing your API specification, take a moment to ask yourself two questions: what problem are you trying to solve, and what is the impact you want to have by building this API? The answers to both of these questions must focus on the needs of the user as well as the business you have created.

The answer to the first question should be succinct enough to state at the top of any product or technical specification. It should include information on how the problem affects or involves the customers and the business.

The answer to the second question should define what success looks like for your API. It should illustrate the desired behaviors you'd like to see from developers who are using your API.

The earlier you ask these questions, the more you will be able to make informed design decisions to achieve your goals.

The following sidebar demonstrates how the problem and impact statements might look for the new MyFiles API.

Problem and Impact Statements for the MyFiles API

Problem

> Our archive repositories provide valuable file metadata to our direct customers. Customers use this data to integrate with business-critical services, but they are currently doing this by downloading CSVs and uploading CSVs to other business products. We are currently not providing a way to programmatically grant access to the archive metadata to customers who use third-party integrations.

Impact

> As a result of building an API, developers creating business integrations for archival metadata will be able to create plug-ins that enhance our product. In addition, existing customers will now be able to use our product in ways that they were not able to before, and therefore they will be more engaged on a daily basis.

In these statements, three key parties are mentioned:

- The MyFiles business
- The customers
- The developers building third-party integrations

Although a three-way relationship is applicable to the MyFiles API, for other businesses, the only parties involved in the problem and impact statements could be the company and the developers, who are also the customers. Use the problem and impact statements to clearly define who the API user is.

After you've done this, make sure there is alignment from other stakeholders at your company. It's important for all parties who will build or use this API to understand the problems that it is trying to solve. Mismatched expectations lead to conflict later on, which can turn into an inconsistent or contradictory API design.

One important reason to define the problem and impact clearly is that when you're starting out with a design proposal, before you've implemented anything, there might be ideological conversations. For example, stakeholders might have a strong opinion about implementation details, such as whether to use RPC or REST and other similar topics. Without being able to focus on the problem statement, your entire company could end up in ideological limbo. A clear statement of the problem and desired impact will help to guide pragmatic choices and designs that are grounded in your users' needs.

As you answer these questions, keep in mind that your API will change if your product does. In the best-case scenario, your API will become a living system that grows as it interacts with other entities across the internet. The "truths" you take for granted today might not be the same as those tomorrow. But don't let this fact stop your design—design for today, and leave a small door to step through for tomorrow.

Even if this isn't your first time designing an API for your product, defining your problem and impact statement is still important. In fact, we believe that it's *even more* important. With an established API and product, developing it is more complicated because of backward compatibility and dependencies on other teams. Do the difficult work up front and make sure you have researched:

- What APIs are available, and what are their patterns and conventions?
- What are the most popular features of the comparable APIs that you have already released? Can you use existing instrumenting or logging to pull supporting metrics?
- What would you most like to change about the APIs that you already have, and what is your strategy for doing so?
- Which other teams will be affected by your new API, and how can you get their feedback early?

Outline Key User Stories

After you outline the problem and desired impact, write down some of the use cases that you expect your API to fulfill. (If you're familiar with Agile methodologies, these will be similar to "user stories," in which the user is your developer.) In any case, you'll want to note the user type and the action that the user will be able to complete. Example 5-1 shows the template.

Example 5-1. Template for Defining Key User Stories

As a [**user type**], I want [**action**] so that [**outcome**].

Example 5-2 presents some examples for our MyFiles API.

Example 5-2. Example User Stories for the MyFiles API, Scenario 1

As a **developer**, I want to **request a list of files** so that **I can see what a user has uploaded.**

As a **developer**, I want to **request details for a single file** so that **I can get details on a file that a user has uploaded.**

As a **developer**, I want to **upload files on behalf of a user** so that **users don't need to leave my app to add a file to MyFiles.**

As a **developer**, I want to **edit files on behalf of a user** so that **users don't need to leave my app to add a file to MyFiles.**

In the next section, we look at how these user stories translate directly into the technology architecture decisions.

Select Technology Architecture

As we mentioned before, modern consumers aren't just looking for products that get the job done. Product design extends beyond the user-friendliness of the actual product to the experience of selecting and receiving it. IKEA has famously created products with simple packaging that are easy to assemble without instructions. Amazon has "hassle-free" shipping. The same developers who expect seamless consumer experiences are also developing against your API. That's why picking the right paradigm and authentication system is so important.

Let's begin by choosing the paradigm for the API you'd like to create. Use what you learned in Chapter 2 to fill out the chart in Table 5-1 with pros and cons of each pattern. Here, we've filled it out for the MyFiles API.

Table 5-1. Pros and cons of different API paradigms for the MyFiles API

Paradigm	Pros	Cons	Selected?
REST	MyFiles is essentially resource-oriented—the resources are the archived content and metadata. The operations to support are simple Create, Read, Update and Delete (CRUD) operations.	REST would be a long-term commitment to a resources model for files. If we need to support several actions, REST might not be a great fit.	✓
RPC	Expandable to other actions beyond CRUD.	At this time, there are no operations outside of CRUD that this API will execute, so there doesn't appear to be a need to support other actions.	✗
GraphQL	Flexible for developers. Easy to keep payloads small.	Overly complicated to implement. No client presentation needed at this time.	✗

For the MyFiles API, the best option based on the pros and cons is REST. The REST pattern closely matches the MyFiles product, which is resource-oriented. We need to give developers access to the MyFiles account from the very beginning so they get a full picture. Let's focus on the build phase of the REST API here in Scenario 1.

In Scenario 2, we'll take a look at how WebHooks offer a mechanism for MyFiles to push data to developers so that they aren't constantly polling the REST API or maintaining open connections with the MyFiles servers.

Now that we've picked our transport, let's pick our authentication mechanism using the MyFiles example and what we learned from Chapter 3. Because some customers have sensitive files, we want something more robust than Basic Authentication and have selected OAuth with short-lived tokens and refresh tokens. This ensures a higher level of security for private files that users might archive. Now that we've selected OAuth, we want to pick some OAuth scopes.

To do this, we need to list the types of resources that we want to provide, along with the operations that will be allowed via the API. After that, we'll fill in a scope scheme that makes sense. For Table 5-2, we will be filling out resources in the left-hand column because the MyFiles API will be REST-based. Your API may be different, and you might want to think about the objects that you'll provide via your API instead of resources. These objects might be data affected by user actions, data affected by developer actions, or any data that you will be transporting to the developer. Notice the close correlation between the operations and CRUD for MyFiles in Table 5-2. Your operations might differ, especially if you have elected a different paradigm, such as RPC.

Table 5-2. Operations and resources for the MyFiles API

Resource or object	Operation
Files and their metadata	Create
Files and their metadata	Read
Files and their metadata	Update
Files and their metadata	Delete

Now that we have resources and operations, it's time to pick our OAuth scopes. We have several options:

- We could create a general scope, `files`, that would cover all operations related to files.
- We could split the files into two buckets of actions: reading and writing.
- We could get even more granular and split the scope into the specific CRUD operations.

After thinking about the scopes and the supported operations more carefully, we decide to eliminate the ability to delete files. That's not an action that users take very often, and it's been identified as the riskiest operation. As a result, for MyFiles, we will have simple `read` and `write` scopes that will cover our three operations. In the MyFiles product, reading is a less risky scope than writing, so we want to be able to distinguish the two for users authorizing applications. At the same time, the two scopes offer the option of being expanded to other operations when we're ready to release them. Table 5-3 shows how that breaks down for our resources.

Table 5-3. Scopes, operations, and resources for the MyFiles API

Resource or object	Operation	Scope
Files and their metadata	Create	`write`
Files and their metadata	Read	`read`
Files and their metadata	Update	`write`

In the MyFiles example, the relationship between decisions and documentation was fairly dynamic. Listing the desired operations and thinking about the OAuth scopes resulted in a hard decision to reduce the initial functionality offering for the API. Decisions about implementation and scope inevitably need to be made during the design process. These decisions should be embraced insomuch as they help better solve the problem that you initially defined.

Write an API Specification

Now that you've made some key high-level decisions, it's time to write a specification (also called a *spec*). The spec gives you an opportunity to think through your design thoroughly. It also serves as an artifact that you can use to communicate with other people, especially when you are soliciting feedback from stakeholders. Finally, after you have reached agreement on the spec, it serves as a contract, enabling you to build the various parts of the API implementation in parallel.

We recommend using collaborative document-editing software with version control and commenting support. This is a great way to boost participation, track feedback, and keep everyone up to date with the latest changes.

The Introduction for the MyFiles API Technical Specification

A strong spec starts off with a high-level summary, detailing major decisions you've made, and a brief explanation of why you made those decisions. The following offers an example of how that might look for MyFiles.

Title
  Proposal: MyFiles API Spec

Authors

Brenda Jin

Saurabh Sahni

Amir Shevat

Problem

Our archive repositories provide valuable file metadata to our direct customers. Customers use this data to integrate with business-critical services, but they are currently doing so by downloading CSVs and uploading CSVs to other business products. We are currently not providing a way to programmatically grant access to the repository metadata to customers who use third-party integrations.

Solution

Build an API that allows developers to programmatically access MyFiles files.

Implementation

For this API, we've decided to use REST for the following reasons:

- REST resource paradigm matches how MyFiles treats files in our tech stack.
- Desired file operations for the API match closely to CRUD operations.
- No need for event transport at this time.

Authentication

This API will use OAuth 2.0 with refresh tokens and token expiry.

Other things we considered

WebHooks are a great way for developers to get information about user events, such as files uploaded and files changed without continuously polling for data. We've decided to incorporate an outline of how these would work. We anticipate building those as a phase 2 for the API.

We have decided not to implement a DELETE operation for third-party developers at this time, because we consider it high risk and unnecessary for the initial API launch.

From there, the spec should dive into increasingly detailed information, such as an outline of the developer's workflow, authentication information (if new authorization mechanisms are being built), and any relevant details about data transmission protocols. Visual diagrams can go a long way toward communicating information that is complex to describe with words.

Tables are also useful tools for detailing multidimensional aspects of APIs. For REST or RPC APIs, it can be helpful to outline the URIs or method names, inputs, outputs, errors, and scope.

Table 5-4 demonstrates what this looks like for our simple MyFiles example.

Table 5-4. Detail section describing each API URI in the MyFiles API technical specification

URI	Inputs	Outputs	Scope

GET
 	
/files
	Required: N/A
	Optional:
	include_deleted (bool)
	default false
	
	limit (int)
	default 100, Max 1000
	
	cursor (string)
	default null
	
	last_updated_after
	(timestamp):
	default null
		200 OK
		Array of $file resources:
		[
		  {
		    "id": $id,
		    "name": string,
		    "date_added":
		      $timestamp,
		    "last_updated":
		      $timestamp,
		    "size": int,
		    "permalink": $uri,
		    "is_deleted": bool
		  }
		]
			read

GET files/:id		200 OK $file	read
PATCH files/:id	Updatable fields: name (string) notes (string)	202 Accepted $file	write
POST files/:id	Required: name (string) Optional: notes (string)	200 Created $file	write

In your table, the *URI* (or *Endpoint*) column should include the HTTP method for REST endpoints. The *Inputs* column should include all input parameters, their acceptable types, their default values, and whether the parameters are required. The *Outputs* column should outline a success response and its types. For the types, you may want to use shorthand values or whatever notations that your use to denote the types throughout your code base. You may also want to specify custom types that you have or will define with an API description language. (For more information on this, see Chapter 7.) Alternatively, you might want to simply include a literal example. The *Errors* column should include any important user errors that you will be exposing for the individual API. You should not document general errors and system errors here. If you're using OAuth, the *Scope* column specifies the scope that grants access to the API method. (See also "API Specification Template" on page 203.)

In the specification of the MyFiles API URIs, we've also added error codes that are specific to each resource. In addition to these resource-specific errors, it's important to think globally about how we will respond with errors that could happen in any API. Table 5-5 includes a list of general and specific errors, along with the HTTP status codes that we've chosen for the MyFiles example in this scenario.

Table 5-5. Section describing HTTP status codes for errors in the MyFiles API technical specification

Status code	Description	Error response body
200 OK	The request succeeded.	See Outputs in Table 5-4.
201 Created	The request succeeded and a new file was created.	See Outputs in Table 5-4.
202 Accepted	The file was updated successfully.	See Outputs in Table 5-4.

400 Bad Request	The request cannot be accepted, often because of a missing parameter or due to an error, like too large a file being given.	`{ "error": "missing_parameter", "message": "The following parameters are missing from your request: <parameter1>, <parameter2>." }`
		
		`{ "error": "file_size_too_large", "message": "The file provided is too large. The limit is <file_size_limit>." }`

Status code	Description	Error response body
401 Unauthorized	No valid access token was provided.	`{ "error": "unauthorized", "message": "The provided token is not valid." }`
403 Forbidden	The user may not have permission to view the file.	`{ "error": "forbidden", "message": "You do not have permission to access the requested file <id>." }`
404 Not Found	The requested file was not found.	`{ "error": "file_not_found", "message": "The requested file <id> was not found." }`
429 Too Many Requests	Too many requests were sent in a given amount of time.	`{ "error": "too_many_requests", "message": "You have made too many requests in a short period of time. Try again in <time> minutes." }`
500 Server Error	Something went wrong on the server side.	

You might notice that there are decisions to make regarding how to note types and resources. Sometimes, you need room to describe which types are nullable and which types are optional. Additionally, you need a place for more information, such as how you would like to handle file uploads via your API. You might want to add a *Notes* column and put that information there. If you run out of horizontal space, you can always turn the page to landscape mode or use a document editor with horizontally scrollable tables.

Beyond what we've already mentioned listing in your API spec, you might also want to include additional information about scaling, performance, logging, and security. Finally, at the end of the spec, it can be useful to include an *Open Questions* section, where you can list unanswered questions.

Scenario 2

Let's take the API design for MyFiles further. Here's the scenario for the next part of the chapter:

You've built and released the MyFiles REST API, and it's been a huge success over the past few months. You've been staying in touch with developers to get their feedback, and you've heard that they want the ability to receive updates when files have changed. With the original REST design, this means that they must make multiple requests on every notable file and check for any kind of difference. This polling behavior is taking a toll on your infrastructure, and it's not user-friendly for developers. As a result, your team has decided to build something to address this problem.

Define the Problem

Here is how how the problem and impact statements might look for Scenario 2:

Problem and Impact Statements for Scenario 2 of the MyFiles API

Problem
> Our REST API has enabled developers to programmatically access third-party integrations. However, the only way developers currently have to keep track of changes to files is by constantly polling our API, up to once per minute per file.

Impact
> After adding some additional features to our API, developers will be able to receive updates whenever changes are made to files they care about.

Outline Key User Stories

"The User Story for the MyFiles API, Scenario 2" on page 73 shows the key user story for Scenario 2.

The User Story for the MyFiles API, Scenario 2

As a **developer**, I want to **receive an update when a file has been added, changed, or removed** so that **I don't have to continuously poll the REST API**.

Select Technology Architecture

In Scenario 1, we selected a REST API for our technical architecture. In this scenario, we are considering a variety of event-driven APIs. Table 5-6 lays out the pros and cons of three common patterns for the MyFiles API: WebHooks, WebSockets, and HTTP Streaming.

 If you need a refresher on the various types of event-driven APIs, head back to Chapter 2.

Table 5-6. Pros and cons of event-driven API paradigms for the MyFiles API

Paradigm	Pros	Cons	Selected?
WebHooks	MyFiles developers might want to receive an event every time files are added, removed, or changed.	If files are changing too frequently, we might need sophisticated infrastructure to deduplicate events so that we don't inadvertently initiate distributed denial-of-service (DDoS) events on our developers' applications.	✓
WebSockets	Can be used by internal clients for UI display.	We don't want developers creating UI clients for MyFiles via the API. We don't believe there is a use case to support long-lived connections for the types of events that developers would want to know about.	✗
HTTP Streaming	Good for pushing data frequently.	With the low frequency of changes per file, we don't see a need for HTTP Streaming.	✗

Based on the pros and cons of the various styles of event-driven APIs, we've decided to select WebHooks. One additional aspect of this design that you should consider is how developers are going to configure their settings to select exactly which events and files they're interested in. Keep that in mind, but we won't get into the configuration design in this chapter.

Write an API Specification

Now, taking the key user story and the selected technology architecture into account, refer to the following example spec for the MyFiles WebHooks design. If you're following along with your own example, you might want to use the API Specification Template provided ("API Specification Template" on page 203).

Sample Spec for the MyFiles WebHooks Design for Scenario 2

Title

Proposal: MyFiles API WebHooks Spec

Authors

Brenda Jin

Saurabh Sahni

Amir Shevat

Problem

Our REST API has enabled developers to programmatically access third-party integrations. However, the only way developers currently have to keep track of changes to files is by constantly polling our API, up to once per minute per file.

Solution

Build an event-driven WebHooks API that allows developers to receive selected add, update, and change events relating to MyFiles files.

Implementation

Developers will specify an endpoint that they control for our WebHooks to send POST requests with JSON bodies for each spec. See Table 5-7 for payload specification.

Authentication

This API will use the OAuth 2.0 authentication from the MyFiles REST API. Any developer who has installed the read OAuth scope will be able to receive WebHook requests.

Other things we considered

There are a number of ways to design event-driven APIs, and we elected WebHooks. WebSockets and long-lived HTTP streaming connections were also considered.

In addition to the high-level overview, let's also write details about the events and their payloads. Table 5-7 shows how that could look.

Table 5-7. Section describing event objects for the MyFiles API technical specification

Event	Payload	OAuth scope

file_added	{
	  "id": $id,
	  "resource_type":
	  "file",
	  "event_type": "added",
	  "name": string,
	  "date_added": $timestamp,
	  "last_updated": $timestamp,
	  "size": int,
	  "permalink": $uri,
	  "notes": array <file_notes>,
	  "uri": $uri
	}
		read

file_changed	{
	  "id": $id,
	  "resource_type": "file",
	  "event_type": "changed",
	  "name": string,
	  "date_added": $timestamp,
	  "last_updated": $timestamp,
	  "size": int,
	  "permalink": $uri,
	  "notes": array <file_notes>,
	  "uri": $uri
	}
		read

file_removed	{
	  "id": $id,
	  "resource_type": "file",
	  "event_type": "removed",
	  "name": string,
	  "date_added": $timestamp,
	  "last_updated": $timestamp,
	  "size": null,
	  "permalink": null,
	  "notes": null,
	  "uri": null
	}
		read

Notice that in this example there are interesting decisions to be made about how to note the type of change for this particular resource. Should there be more data in the payload? Or should the event names be granular, with references to where developers can make a subsequent request, and get more information, as described by the payload.uri field in Table 5-7?

Validate Your Decisions

Now that we've explored how to write an API specification, it's time to get feedback. After each specification is written, you should find a way to test your ideas with stakeholders. In this chapter, we have provided two different specs to give a range of examples, but in the real world there would be time between each of these scenarios, and feedback would be solicited after each specification was written. Don't wait to finish building your API masterpiece before getting input—the right feedback early on can save you a lot of time and prevent costly rewrites.

Reviewing the specification with stakeholders

One of the guiding principles of the design methodology described in this chapter is enabling feedback early and often. The spec you have just written is a starting point for much of this, where you can get feedback on the problem, the high-level solution, and the nitty-gritty details. Review your spec with others and solicit feedback on the design. Find a developer who might build a business integration and ask them what they think. If your stakeholders are internal, make sure that you get their input. It is important to go through these cycles of feedback before you write any code because the mindsets for creating and consuming an API are different, and the input you receive will help you fix usability issues before you start building.

The point of gathering feedback is not to simply "get sign-off." As you are gathering feedback, you should be inviting constructive disagreement and criticism. This isn't so that others can tear down your design but so that you can collect valuable information to improve it before you begin building. (Hopefully you have relationships with key stakeholders that are built on trust and mutual understanding to help move this conversation along.)

Gathering feedback is not an effort to prove (or disprove) your design prowess. In fact, it isn't even about your ideas. It should be an authentic exploration of the possible solutions to the problem you defined at the beginning of this chapter. Genuine curiosity throughout the feedback cycle enables the exchange of ideas. When gathering feedback, you should be deepening your understanding of other stakeholders' concerns and hesitations, even if they're difficult to hear and even if you disagree. When phrasing questions, it's better to be specific about the information you'd like. For example, "Did you like it?" isn't as helpful as "What problems did you run into as you implemented the WebHooks API?" You might even ultimately decide not to incorporate some of your stakeholders' suggestions because your solution addresses their concerns another way. With this deeper understanding, your solutions will be more thorough and more multifaceted, and you will make more intentional trade-offs.

It certainly takes effort to synthesize complex ideas and merge seemingly disparate interests—it's more work than simply running with your first solution. However, it's better to build the right API than to build the wrong one.

Mocking data for interactive user testing

We recommend using whatever tools are available to you in order to test your design and gather the feedback you need. One of the tools you might want to use is mock data. For example, you could create an interface for developers in which they can get mock data in the format of your proposed spec. The mock data is a set of fixed responses that can be served through an application or some other lightweight interface that you can route through your existing web application. The mock data application will be a more interactive testing environment for stakeholders, which will help you get even more specific feedback before you fully implement the API. Additionally, a mocking tool can help your developers implement their apps and integrations in parallel with your API development.

Storytime: Macys.com Responsive Checkout

In 2015, Macys.com built a brand-new responsive checkout system that used a series of JSON APIs. The previous system was built as individual pages on a Java backend using the Spring Framework. Because it was going to take several weeks for the backend developers to create the JSON API, the team first agreed upon the API spec. Then, the frontend developers created a lightweight Node.js mock application that served fake fixed responses while the API was being developed. This allowed the interactive responsive frontend experience to be built and tested, in parallel with the development of the APIs. When it came time to release the checkout experience to customers, the team simply swapped out the Node.js mock application with the new API endpoints.

Beta testers

Often your stakeholders aren't just internal. If you have a public-facing API, there are also external stakeholders to consider when soliciting feedback. After you make some decisions based on the spec and begin building the API, you'll want to consider getting feedback from developer partners in a beta testing program. This would allow developer partners early access to the new API, with the intent that they would provide feedback before an official public release. This gives you as the API builder additional opportunities to improve the API design for real users and real use cases. For more on building developer partner programs, see Chapter 10.

Closing Thoughts

We think the MyFiles API is off to a good start—don't you? This process provided a generic template for you to use to design APIs. As you think about how to customize the design process for your API, consider keeping the process as *lightweight* and fast as possible, while maximizing the *feedback*.

Throughout this book, we continue to encourage you to think about the human factor in computing. Time and time again, we've seen that poor design decisions are made when API providers ignore the needs of the user or developer communites.

Adapt the template provided here as needed for your organization, but don't forget the user!

CHAPTER 6

Scaling APIs

Making sure your API scales both in terms of use cases and load is critical for its success. In this section, we cover the following scaling best practices and tips to help ensure that your API is future-proof:

- Scaling throughput
- Evolving API design
- Paginating APIs
- Rate-limiting APIs
- Developer SDKs

When you are building an API that other people depend on, availability and reliability are important. You want to ensure that it never goes down and that it continues to load fast for its users. However, your API can suddenly experience a surge in usage. That can affect the quality of your service or even bring your own application down, if the application relies on your APIs.

To scale your API by supporting an increased number of API calls, there are many things you can do at the application level. Database query optimization, sharding databases, adding missing indexes, utilizing caching, doing expensive operations asynchronously, writing efficient code, and tuning web servers help in increasing the throughput and decreasing the latency. All of these things are very important and you should do them. We cover these topics only briefly in the first section of this chapter, given that they are covered more extensively in other books about web application performance.

Beyond these optimizations, there is another set of changes that are frequently overlooked and can significantly help in scaling APIs. There are ways in which you can develop your API design, change API usage policies, or help third-party developers to write efficient code when working with your API. In "Evolving Your API Design" on page 90, we cover these often-forgotten best practices and tips that can be useful for scaling your API.

Your API might also need to handle increasingly large datasets. Pagination is an effective strategy for delivering large datasets to developers. We go over some tips and techniques for this in "Paginating APIs" on page 97.

Even after you have taken care of all the aforementioned concerns by scaling your throughput, developing your API design, and paginating your APIs, it's still possible for developers to make requests at an overwhelmingly high rate. In "Rate-Limiting APIs" on page 102, we discuss strategies for effectively limiting developer requests to a reasonable frequency to maintain the health of your overall application.

Finally, scaling APIs isn't just about the mechanisms within your application and API that enable growth. In "Developer SDKs" on page 114, we discuss how to create tools for developers to encourage best practices.

Scaling Throughput

As the number of users of an API grows, the throughput—measured as the number of API calls per second—increases. In this section, we talk about various ways in which you can optimize your API to support this growth.

Finding the Bottlenecks

Scaling your API might require fundamental changes to your application architecture and code. First, you need to determine what your scaling bottlenecks are; otherwise, you're just making guesses. One of the best ways to gain insights into bottlenecks is through instrumentation. By collecting data on usage and monitoring for capacity bottlenecks, you can take advantage of data-driven insights into optimizations that will help you scale.

Generally, these bottlenecks fall into four categories:

Disk I/O
Expensive database queries and local disk access often lead to disk-related bottlenecks.

Network I/O
Network bottlenecks in modern applications are frequently caused by dependencies on external services requiring API calls across data centers.

CPU
Inefficient code performing expensive computations is one of the common causes of CPU bottlenecks.

Memory
Memory bottlenecks typically occur when systems do not have sufficient RAM.

Most of the cloud hosting providers offer solutions to measure these bottlenecks. If you're on Amazon Web Services (AWS), you can use Amazon CloudWatch. Heroku has New Relic. And on Google, you can use Stackdriver to access metrics and get insights into health, performance, and availability.

To pinpoint specific bottlenecks, you can monitor the categories we just listed, homing in on your most frequently called API methods. One of the most obvious symptoms of a bottleneck is high latency for response times. By measuring the response times of your API methods and how frequently they are called, you can narrow down the methods you want to optimize.

After you determine which API methods to optimize, performance profiling is one of the best ways to identify your bottlenecks. Although performance and scaling are different, they are related. Poorly performing APIs are difficult to scale.

By profiling your code, you can find out which are your CPU- or memory-intensive functions. Profiling in a development environment often helps you to find the application bottlenecks; however, sometimes the issues in production are different. This is especially true if activities and events that happen in production are difficult to simulate or reproduce in your development environment. If you enable profiling in production for a small subset of your traffic, you can gain further insights into the performance issues. Figure 6-1 shows Stackdrivers that help engineers understand which paths consume the most resources and the different ways in which their code is actually called.

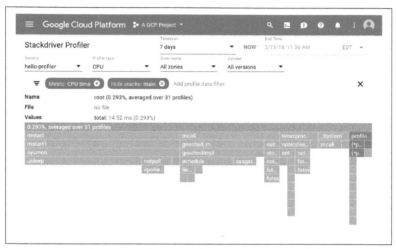

Figure 6-1. Performance flame graph generated by Stackdriver Profiler in Google Cloud Platform

In addition to code profiling, which identifies CPU- or memory-intensive functions, database profiling helps you to pinpoint the slow queries related to disk I/O. MySQL offers a slow query log that can log queries that take a long time to execute. Other databases offer similar solutions to analyze and isolate potentially problematic queries.

As for network I/O bottlenecks, load testing, along with the aforementioned methods, is another commonly used technique to determine how your API will behave under anticipated peak load conditions. Load testing is helpful in identifying the maximum operating capacity of a system as well as bottlenecks that can lead to service degradation at high load. Some companies use load testing to perform internal drills in advance of known upcoming spikes. Notably, ecommerce companies do this to prepare and plan in advance for spikes—of up to five times the traffic and transactions—that can occur during major shopping events, such as Black Friday in the United States.

Adding Computing Resources

Simply adding more computing resources can help in scaling an application. There are two ways to add more resources:

Vertical scaling
> Vertical scaling can be achieved by adding more power, like CPUs, RAM, and disk storage, to existing servers.

Horizontal scaling
> Horizontal scaling is achieved by adding more server instances to your pool of resources so that the load can be distributed among them.

Figure 6-2 shows the architecture of a typical large web application. Web servers are fronted by a load balancer distributing requests across servers. To horizontally scale databases, data is often partitioned such that rows of a database table are stored on different servers. Each server contains only part of the data. This is also referred to as *database sharding*. Along with sharding, *database replication* is used to distribute the load on the database. This is helpful in improving performance, reliability, and scalability. There are many nuances to scaling cloud application architecture which we won't cover in this book.

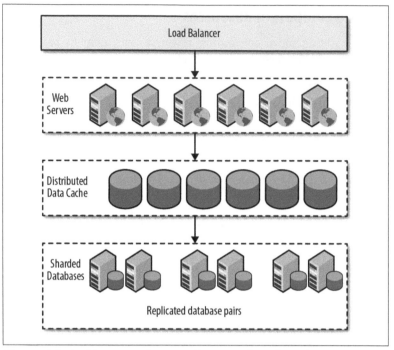

Figure 6-2. Architecture of a typical large-scale web application

Database Indexes

Indexing is a way to optimize the performance of data retrieval operations on a database table. Indexes help databases to locate rows to return for a query without having to compare every row in a database table. They do this by additionally storing the index data structure.

For example, if you frequently find users by email address in a users table, creating an index on the email column will help you to speed up these queries. Without an index, the database would need to examine every row.

However, adding too many indexes is not ideal, either. Each index on a table requires additional storage space, and there is a performance hit every time you add, update, or delete rows because the corresponding indexes need to be updated as well. Typically, you need indexes on columns that are common in your WHERE, ORDER BY, and GROUP BY clauses.

For more information on implementing database indexes, consult the documentation and resources for your specific database.

Caching

Caching is one of the most popular and simplest techniques that web applications use to scale to very large throughput. Caching solutions like Memcached store data in memory instead of on the disk because it is much faster to read from memory.

Caching is often used to store the responses to database queries. By analyzing your database logs, you can figure out the database queries that take a long time to execute and are most frequent. With caching, when you need to look up data, you first check whether it's available in the cache. If you find the data, you return it. Otherwise, you can do a database query to find results and store them in the cache for future lookups before returning the response to the user. By caching these results in memory, you can significantly improve the scalability and performance of your application.

When you implement caching, one important thing to remember is to invalidate the cache. Often you want to delete the cache whenever the corresponding data is updated. At other times, when you can tolerate data update delays, you might let the cache expire on its own.

Although application-level caching for APIs is typically implemented along with your web servers, caching API results closer to end users can help to achieve even higher throughput and performance. This is referred to as *edge caching*.

Storytime: Slack's Flannel—an Application-Level Edge Cache

In the early days of Slack, the Slack clients used a very different API design than they eventually would (see Figure 6-3). In this context, a client is any application used to display the messages and other features of Slack, including web browsers and native desktop and mobile applications. When Slack was used primarily on small teams, each client would make an API request to load everything on startup. This was useful for getting all the channels, users, and bots to display at once.

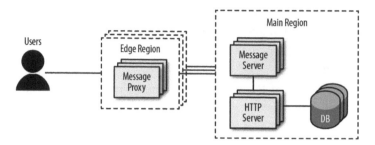

Figure 6-3. Slack's pre-Flannel architecture

However, as teams grew larger and larger, requesting the entire state of the application became slow. What had worked for small teams didn't work for large teams. Connection time to start took too long, the client memory footprint became too big, reconnecting to Slack were expensive, and reconnection storms became resource-intensive.

As a result, Slack spent months redesigning the API for clients to request and manage state. This API became known as *Flannel*. As Figure 6-4 illustrates, Flannel was a lazy-loading cache service that provided query APIs for clients to fetch data on demand. Whereas previously, clients received the entire application state on startup, they now used Flannel to request only what they needed to create a reasonable user interface (UI) for human users and then made subsequent requests to update their local state.

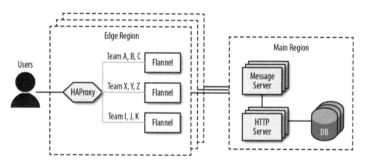

Figure 6-4. Slack's architecture with Flannel

It took a whole team and months of work to get this new cache in place to scale the API, but the results were phenomenal. Client startup data size was reduced by 7 times on a medium-sized team and 44 times on a large team. For more information on this story, see the Slack engineering blog (*http://bit.ly/2w160iU*).

Doing Expensive Operations Asynchronously

If some of your API requests take a long time to execute, you might want to consider performing expensive operations outside of the request (*asynchronously*). This way you can serve the responses to such requests faster.

For example, if you have a system that allows users to store and search files, when a file is uploaded, you do not need to make it available in the search index as part of the same request. Files can be added to the index as part of an offline job that's executed asynchronously in near real time.

To do operations asynchronously, you can use task queue services provided by various cloud service providers, like Amazon and Google. You can also use an open source task queue like Celery.

Scaling Throughput Best Practices

Here are some best practices that will help your applications to scale to high load:

- Measure and find your bottlenecks first before starting to make changes for scaling. The database is the most common bottleneck in modern applications.

- Avoid premature optimizations. Scaling optimizations often come at a cost, and some of them can increase the development time of your application. Unless you have scaling problems, you probably don't want to add that complexity.

- Prefer horizontal scalability over vertical scalability.

- Understand that database indexes are among the best ways to address slow database queries.

- Determine which data you use frequently, and cache it.

- If you add caching, do not forget to add cache invalidation.

- Consider performing expensive operations asynchronously.

- Avoid writing inefficient code that might do expensive operations, like database queries in a `for` loop for a single API request.

Evolving Your API Design

In the real world, your initial API design might not scale with the growth of your user base or with the increased adoption and usage of your API. For insights into bottlenecks that may occur and to reduce the number of API calls, it's important to determine the main reasons that developers are using the API and where the issues are. Are developers using the API for reasons you didn't predict? Is polling a problem? Is the API returning too much data? Although there is no magic bullet to resolve all scaling issues, you may want to consider the following solutions.

Expert Advice

Grow and work with your users. Keep a good and open channel with your developers/users. Gain feedback and tune the API to solve their main pain points.

—Ido Green, developer advocate at Google

Introducing New Data Access Patterns

As your API becomes popular, your developers might begin using it in ways that you didn't anticipate. To address scaling challenges, you might want to consider alternative ways of sharing data. Let's take a look at four companies that took on significant API design changes in order to scale: Zapier, Twitter, GitHub, and Slack.

If polling is one of your API scaling problems and you have only REST APIs, you should explore options like WebSockets and WebHooks. Your developers will not need to poll for changes but can wait for new data to be delivered in real time. A 2013 Zapier study (*https://zapier.com/engineering/introducing-resthooksorg/*) found that only about 1.5% of their polling API calls returned new data. By supporting WebHooks, they estimated that server load could be reduced by 66 times.

In the past, Twitter applications could only receive new tweets in near real time by frequently polling the Twitter API. This led to increased traffic to the REST APIs, and as a result, added to existing scaling challenges. To resolve the issue, Twitter introduced a streaming API that delivers new data and cuts down on polling. Now, using this streaming API, developers can subscribe to selected keywords or users and can receive new tweets over a long-lived connection.

In the past, GitHub found that its responses were bloated and were sending too much data but even with the large payloads, they still weren't including all of the data that developers needed. Developers would make separate calls to assemble a complete view of a resource. To address these scalability challenges, GitHub launched the GraphQL API (*https://githubengineering.com/the-github-graphql-api/*). Using GraphQL, developers can batch multiple API calls into a single API call and fetch only the items that they needed. This helps to reduce the number of API calls GitHub receives, and it reduces the cost of computation on fields that developers don't need.

Slack started out with a Real-Time Messaging (RTM) API, which allowed developers to build apps and bots that could respond in real time to activities in Slack. The API delivered events from Slack over a WebSocket. As time went on, Slack discovered that even though the RTM API was great for its own clients, it provided too much data for developers to handle well. Plus, it was difficult for Slack and for developers to scale. Developers with several users had to deal with many concurrent open HTTP connections—at least one per user. Slack also needed to manage as many connections as the API provider. In 2016, to address all of these problems, Slack introduced the Events API (Figure 6-5), which is WebHook-based and enables developers to create bots over HTTP. Instead of receiving an endless stream of data that includes all events, and rather than constantly polling Slack's RPC API, developers can use the Events API to subscribe to only the events that they care about—delivered via HTTP. This helps both Slack and app developers to scale better.

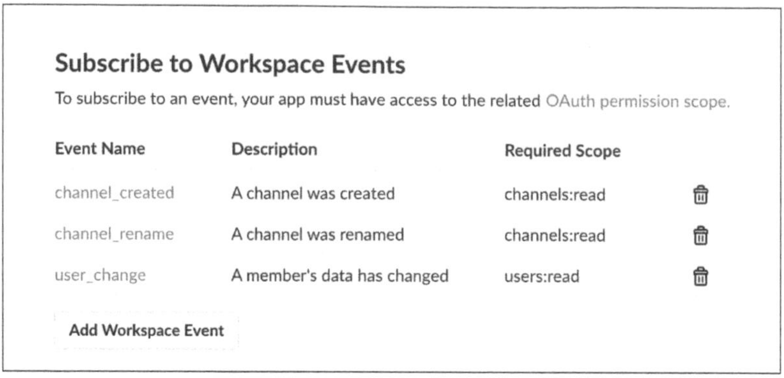

Figure 6-5. Slack's WebHook-based event subscription interface

Adding New API Methods

Another way to address scalability and performance problems is by adding new API methods. If you have some expensive APIs, you might want to dive deeper into the use cases they are serving. Sometimes developers might need only a small subset of the data from your API responses, or, as in the GitHub case that we just looked at, developers might be working hard to assemble data that isn't easily accessible with the existing APIs. If developers can only either request everything or nothing, they may end up receiving full responses and ignoring most of the payloads. It's possible that the data they don't need is expensive for you to compute. It's difficult to remove or change APIs after they are in use, but adding new methods is easy. New methods can deliver the data that your developers need, while addressing the performance and scale issues of your existing APIs.

Slack introduced several new APIs over time to address scaling challenges. One of Slack's popular API methods, `rtm.start`, became extremely expensive. This method would start an RTM session and return a wide variety of data about the team, its channels, and its members. Originally designed for small teams, this API method would return the full application state, in addition to a session URL for a WebSocket connection. As team sizes grew, this payload became unwieldy and large—up to several megabytes, which was expensive for developers to handle. Even though a handful of developers used the data returned from this method, most developers wanted only to connect to the WebSocket. As a result, Slack introduced a new API method, `rtm.connect`, that simply returns an

RTM WebSocket API session URL without returning any other data in the payload. This new method has helped application developers and Slack to overcome some of the scaling problems with rtm.start.

Slack also launched a new Conversations API that addresses performance and scalability issues along with various developer pain points. Previously, developers needed to use different methods from multiple "family trees" to achieve the same thing, depending on the type of the channel with which they were working. For example, to list private channels, developers would use groups.list, and for public channels, they used channels.list. This resulted in many different objects for developers to reconcile—objects that, at their core, all represented the same type of timeline message container. The Conversations API (Figure 6-6) bring consistency to these payloads and addresses various performance improvements so that developers can scale their applications. API endpoints returning lists of large objects are all paginated. Slack also stopped returning large nested lists of lists in payloads and created separate endpoints to fetch additional information. For instance, a new API endpoint, conversations.members, returns a paginated list of members in a conversation. Apart from making Slack's application infrastructure more scalable, these new APIs also make third-party developers' lives much easier. Slack's developers report removing many lines of code (*https://blog.frame.ai/migrating-to-the-slack-conversations-api-89692b016eea*) with this new change.

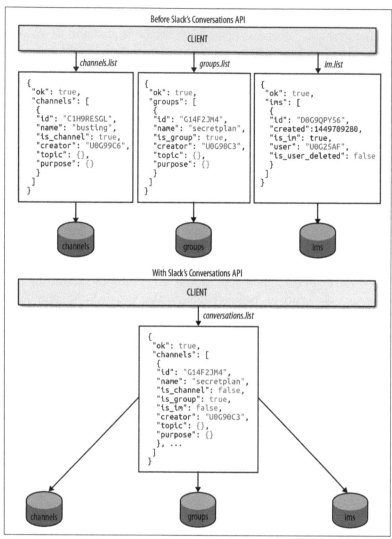

Figure 6-6. Slack's Conversations API consolidated multiple endpoints into one

Another use case that the Conversations API helped developers to complete was that of finding conversations of which a user was a member. To do that, developers would make multiple requests to query the members of each conversation and then filter conversations for a given user. By releasing an API method called `users.con versations`, Slack reduced the number of calls that developers needed to make. In a single request to the new `users.conversa` tions API method, developers could fetch up to 1,000 conversations of which a user was a member. Previously, this could have taken 1,001 API calls.

Supporting Bulk Endpoints

Sometimes developers need to do the same operation on several items, like looking up or updating multiple users. This often requires doing several individual API calls. Supporting bulk endpoints so that developers can do those operations in fewer API calls can be helpful for scaling. Bulk endpoints are more efficient because they require fewer HTTP round trips and can even help in reducing load on a database.

Let's look at another example from Slack. To invite multiples users to a single Slack channel, developers had to call the channels.invite API method once per user. Slack added support for inviting multiple users in a single API call (Example 6-1), thereby saving costs for both Slack and developers. Several API providers, like Zendesk and Salesforce, support bulk operation endpoints as well as batching of requests.

Example 6-1. Slack's Conversations API supporting bulk operations

```
POST /api/conversations.invite
HOST slack.com
Content-Type: application/json
Authorization: Bearer xoxp-165018607-jqf4sbdaq2a
{
  "channel":"C0GEV71UG",
  "users":["W1234567890","U2345678901", "U3456789012"]
}
```

Adding New Options to Filter Results

When your API begins returning a number of objects, it's important to consider providing options to filter the results. This way, developers can limit the number of objects returned to those that they actually need. This makes your API more scalable. Different APIs need different filters depending on how they are used. Here are some common filters that are widely applicable:

Search filter

With search filters, developers can specifically request the results they are looking for using similar words, regex, or matching strings. In the absence of such a filter, developers could end up requesting and parsing a lot more results than they need.

Date filter

Often developers need only new results since the last time they requested results from the API. By supporting a date filter, you can return only the results from after or before the given time-stamp. The Twitter timeline, the Facebook News Feed, and the Slack message history APIs support such filters.

Order filter

An order filter enables developers to order a set of results by a given property. This can reduce the number of results that developers need to request and process. The Amazon Product Advertising API supports sorting by popularity, price, and con-dition.

Options to indicate which fields to return or not return

Some fields in your API responses might be far more expensive to compute than others. Unnecessary fields can also significantly increase the response payload size. API providers frequently offer developers an option to exclude or include certain fields. For example, the Twitter timeline API provides filters to trim included user objects and not return tweets.

Expert Advice

Evolving the API design has helped Facebook and app developers with scaling. Previously, app developers had to include a full Facebook SDK in their mobile apps. Recently, we released an update to our mobile SDKs that allows developers to install certain pieces of it. If a developer does not need the functionality of the full Android SDK, they can save space by using only the SDK(s) needed to support the Facebook products.

—Desiree Motamedi Ward, head of developer product marketing at Facebook

---

Evolving API Design Best Practices

Here are four best practices for evolving API design that will help you with scaling:

- As you continue to evolve your APIs, it's important to ensure that you do not introduce surprising breaking changes to your developers.
- Analyze your API usage and patterns to figure out what to optimize.
- Talk to your developers and partners. This will give you good insights into problems and potential solutions.
- Before launching new API patterns for everyone, try them out with a handful of developers and partners. This way, you can iterate on the design based on their feedback before making the patterns generally available.

Paginating APIs

In addition to scaling throughput and evolving your API design, paginating APIs can help with scaling. Quite often, APIs need to handle large datasets. An API call might end up returning thousands of items. Returning too many items can overload the web application backend and even slow down clients that can't handle large datasets. For that reason, it's important to *paginate* large result sets. This splits long lists of data into smaller chunks, minimizes response times for requests, and makes responses easier to handle.

In this section, we explore some techniques that you can use to paginate an API.

Offset-Based Pagination

Using limits and offsets is generally the easiest way to implement pagination. It's also the most widely used pagination technique.

To paginate this way, clients provide a page size that defines the maximum number of items to return and a page number that indicates the starting position in the list of items. Based on these values, servers storing data in a SQL database can easily construct a query to fetch results. For instance, to fetch the fifth page of items with each page's size being 10, we should load 10 items, starting after 40 items (skipping the first 4 pages of size 10). The corresponding SQL query would look like the following:

```
SELECT * FROM `items`
ORDER BY `id` asc
LIMIT 10 OFFSET 40;
```

APIs, such as GitHub's, support this kind of pagination. Clients can simply make a request with page and per_page parameters specified in the URL, such as the one shown here:

```
https://api.github.com/user/repos?page=5&per_page=10
```

Advantages and disadvantages

Offset-based pagination is extremely simple to implement, both for clients and the server. It also has user experience advantages. It allows users to jump into any arbitrary page instead of forcing them to scroll through the entire content (Figure 6-7).

Previous   1   2   3   Next

Figure 6-7. Pagination links in a UI

However, this technique has a few disadvantages:

- It's inefficient for large datasets. SQL queries with large offsets are pretty expensive. The database has to count and skip rows up to the offset value before it gets to returning the desired set of items.

- It can be unreliable when the list of items changes frequently. The addition of an item while a client is paginating through results could cause the client to display the same item twice. Similarly, on the removal of an item, a client might end up skipping it at the boundary.

- Offset-based pagination can be tricky in a distributed system. For large offsets, you might need to scan a number of shards before you get to the desired set of items.

That said, offset paginations can be great when pagination depth is limited and clients can tolerate duplicates or missed items.

Cursor-Based Pagination

To address the problems of offset-based pagination, various APIs have adopted a technique called *cursor-based pagination*. To use this technique, clients first send a request while passing only the desired number of items. The server then responds with the requested number of items (or the maximum number of items supported and available), in addition to a next cursor. In the subsequent request, along with the number of items, clients pass this cursor indicating the starting position for the next set of items.

Implementing cursor-based pagination is not very different from offset-based pagination. However, it's much more efficient. Systems that store data in a SQL database can create queries based on the cursor values and retrieve results.

Suppose that a server returns a Unix timestamp of the last record as the cursor. To fetch a page of results that are older than that given cursor, the server can construct a SQL query like the following:

```
SELECT * FROM items
WHERE created_at < 1507876861
ORDER BY created_at
LIMIT 10;
```

Having an index on the column `created_at` in the preceding example makes the query fast.

Several modern APIs, including those of Slack, Stripe, Twitter, and Facebook, offer cursor-based pagination. Let's take a look at how cursor-based pagination works in the Twitter API.

Consider this scenario: a developer wants to obtain the list of a user's followers' IDs. To fetch the first page of results, the developer makes an API request, as shown here:

```
GET https://api.twitter.com/1.1/followers/ids.json?screen_name=
    saurabhsahni&count=50
```

The Twitter API returns the following response:

```
{
    "ids": [
        385752029,
        602890434,
```

```
        ...
    333181469,
    333165023
  ],
    ...

    "next_cursor": 1374004777531007833,
}
```

Using the value from next_cursor, the developer can then request the next page of results with the following request:

```
GET https://api.twitter.com/1.1/followers/ids.json?user_id=12345
    &count=50&cursor=1374004777531007833
```

As the developer makes subsequent requests to advance through the next pages, they will eventually receive a response with "next_cursor" as 0, and that will indicate the end of the entire paginated result set.

Advantages and disadvantages

Cursor-based pagination addresses both the issues seen with offset-based pagination:

Performance
One of the key benefits of cursor-based pagination is performance. With an index on the column used in the cursor for pagination, even queries requiring scanning large tables are fast.

Consistency
The addition or removal of items does not affect the result set of a page. While paginating across results, the server returns every item exactly once.

Cursor-based pagination is great for large and dynamic datasets. However, it has a few drawbacks:

- Clients cannot jump to a given page. They need to traverse through the entire result set page by page.

- The results must be sorted on a unique and sequential database column, used for the cursor value. It should not be possible to add records at a random position in the list.

- Implementing cursor-based pagination is a bit more complicated than offset-based pagination, particularly for clients. Clients often need to store the cursor value to use it in subsequent requests.

Choosing what goes in the cursor

Common options to use for cursors include:

ID as the cursor

API providers often choose a unique ID as the cursor value. For instance, the Twitter timeline APIs support tweet IDs as cursors. To fetch older tweets in a timeline, developers can pass the lowest ID received in the first set of results as the `max_id` parameter. The server then returns only tweets with IDs lower than or equal to the value of the `max_id` parameter.

Timestamp

Another common approach adopted by APIs returning time-based data, such as news feeds, is to use the timestamp as the cursor. Facebook APIs support `until` and `since` parameters, which accept Unix timestamps. When a timestamp is passed in the `since` request parameter, the Facebook API returns only items newer than the given timestamp.

Opaque strings

Using opaque strings as the cursor is increasingly becoming the preferred choice for API providers. Although they appear as random sets of characters, they are generally encoded values. A key advantage of using opaque strings is the ability to encode additional information within a single cursor. Large-scale applications can encode multiple IDs or an ID-plus-pointer combination to a database shard in these cursor values. Modern versions of various APIs, including those of Slack, Facebook, GitHub, and Twitter, use opaque strings as cursors.

Pro Tip

Cursor-based pagination is best suited for high-traffic applications for which clients need to scan through large datasets.

Pagination Best Practices

Here are some best practices that you should keep in mind when designing pagination for an API:

- When implementing pagination, do not forget to set reasonable default and maximum values for the page size.
- Avoid using offset-based pagination if clients will run queries with large offsets.
- With pagination, sorting data such that newer items are returned first and older items later is sometimes better. This way clients don't need to paginate through to the end if they are interested only in newer items.
- If your API does not support pagination today, introduce it later in a way that maintains backward compatibility. More on backward compatibility in Chapter 7.
- When implementing pagination, return the next page URL pointing to the subsequent page of results. An empty or null next page value can indicate the end of the list. By encouraging clients to follow the next page URL, over time you can change your pagination strategy without breaking clients.
- Do not encode any sensitive information inside cursors. Clients can generally decode them.

Rate-Limiting APIs

Often API providers discover the need to rate-limit APIs the hard way. When an API becomes popular and suddenly sees a surge of traffic that potentially affects the availability of the application, API developers begin exploring rate-limiting options. There are two key reasons why APIs should do rate-limiting:

To protect the infrastructure while increasing reliability and availability of the application

You do not want a single misbehaving developer or user to bring your application down through a denial-of-service (DoS) attack.

To protect your product
>You want to prevent abuses of your product, like mass registration of users or creation of a lot of spam content.

Rate limits help to handle surges in traffic or spam by making your application more reliable. By safeguarding your infrastructure and product, rate limits are also protecting developers. There is no API or data for anyone if it's possible to bring down the entire system via the API. So, let's dive into what rate-limiting is and how you can implement it for your API.

What Is Rate-Limiting?

A rate-limiting system controls the rate of traffic sent or received on a network interface. For web APIs, rate-limiting systems are used to control how many times an application or a client is allowed to call an API during a given time interval. Traffic is allowed up to the specified rate, whereas traffic that exceeds that rate might be denied. For example, GitHub's API allows developers to make up to 5,000 requests per hour.

When you're thinking about rate-limiting an API, one of the first things you need to do is to come up with a policy. Apart from protecting your infrastructure and product, a good rate-limiting policy has the following characteristics:

- Easy to understand, explain, and work with
- Ensures that developers are not rate-limited while working with desired use cases

Here are a few things to consider when developing your rate-limiting policy:

Granular rate limits versus a global rate limit
>Many APIs choose a single global API rate limit across all API endpoints. This is easy to implement for you as well as for developers. However, if some of your API endpoints consume significantly more resources than others, you might want to define rate limits per endpoint. Such granular rate limits will protect your infrastructure from any unreasonable spikes for an expensive API endpoint. The Twitter API defines a rate limit per API endpoint, whereas GitHub and Facebook define a single global API rate limit.

Measuring traffic per user, application, or client IP

Often the entity which you want to rate-limit depends on the authentication method required by your API. APIs requiring user authentication generally apply rate-limiting on a per-user basis, whereas APIs requiring an application authentication typically rate-limit on a per-app basis. For unauthenticated API calls, API providers often choose to rate-limit by IP address. APIs from GitHub, Facebook, Twitter, and Slack apply rate limits per user for authenticated API calls.

Supporting occasional traffic bursts or not

Some APIs, particularly the ones used by enterprise developers, support traffic bursts beyond a sustained rate limit. This way, developers' applications experiencing a surge in traffic can continue to work well with the API. If you choose to support occasional traffic bursts, you probably want to use the token bucket algorithm to implement rate-limiting. In the next section, we discuss this and other algorithms.

Allowing exceptions

You need not have a single rate-limiting policy or a single set of rate limits (or quota) that are applicable to all your developers. It's possible that some of your trusted developers or partners will need higher rate limits. You can always have exceptions for them, if they request additional quota. That said, before you grant exceptions, you might want to:

- Ensure that the developer's use case is valid and beneficial to customers.

- Verify that there is no better way to achieve the same result with your existing APIs and constraints.

- Validate whether your infrastructure can support the rate limit ask.

Expert Advice

Any API used by external developers requires careful attention to availability, reliability, and security. This is especially true in Stripe's case; payments infrastructure is the lifeblood of our customers' business. One bad actor shouldn't accidentally or deliberately affect its availability.

> We implement a few rate-limiting strategies (*https://stripe.com/blog/rate-limiters*) to prioritize critical requests over noncritical traffic and keep our API available to everyone.
>
> —Romain Huet, head of developer relations at Stripe

Another way to ensure reasonable use of your API is with terms of service (ToS) agreement documentation. These documents detail permitted uses of your API to developers, including rate limits. Developers hitting your API at higher rates than specified in your ToS might be subject to API token invalidation or other actions you deem necessary.

> We address ToS in detail in Chapter 9.

Implementation Strategies

As you build a rate-limiting system, ensure that the system does not slow your API response time. To ensure high performance and the ability to scale horizontally, most API services use in-memory data stores, like Redis and Memcached, to implement the rate-limiter. Both Redis and Memcached offer fast reads and writes and are often used by API providers to keep track of the number of API requests received for rate-limiting.

There are a few common algorithms that are used to implement rate limits:

- Token bucket
- Fixed-window counter
- Sliding-window counter

Token bucket

The token bucket algorithm allows for maintaining a steady upper limit on the rate of traffic while permitting occasional bursts. The algorithm is explained with the analogy of a bucket (Figure 6-8) with finite capacity, into which tokens are added at a fixed rate. But it can't fill up infinitely. If a token arrives when the bucket is full, it's discarded. On every request, n number of tokens are removed from the bucket. If there are fewer than n number of tokens in the bucket, the request is rejected.

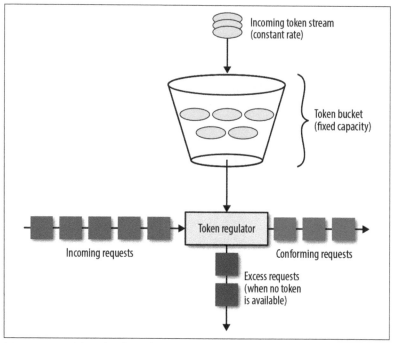

Figure 6-8. Token bucket algorithm

Implementing this algorithm using an in-memory key–value data store is easy. Suppose that you want to rate-limit API requests per user to 20 requests/minute while allowing occasional bursts of up to 50 requests. Here's how a key–value data store implementation could work:

- On the first request for a user, initialize a bucket with the capacity of 50 tokens. Store the request timestamp and this token count in the data store, with the user's identifier as the key.

- On subsequent requests, refill the bucket with new tokens per the defined fixed rate and time elapsed since the last request.

- Then, remove one token from the bucket and update the timestamp to the current timestamp.

- Finally, if the available token count drops to zero, reject the request.

The token bucket algorithm is easy to implement and is used by several API providers, including Slack, Stripe, and Heroku. If you want to be lenient on "bursty" traffic, this is a great choice. Figure 6-9 illustrates how the token bucket algorithm would rate-limit traffic in practice.

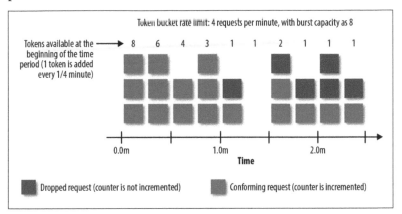

Figure 6-9. Token bucket rate-limiting in practice

Fixed-window counter

The fixed-window counter algorithm allows a fixed number of requests to go through the system over a specified time interval. You can easily implement the fixed window by using an in-memory key–value data store. Implementing a per-user rate limit of 20 requests/minute could work, as described here:

- On the first request, store the request count as 1 for a key representing the user and timestamp rounded to the current minute value. This key can expire after the current minute is over.

- Increment the aforementioned request count key by one on every subsequent request.

- If the request count exceeds the rate limit, reject the request.

Although this is easy to implement, this algorithm can allow up to twice the specified number of requests within the one-minute window. For instance, if there were 20 requests for a user at 11:01:40 a.m., the client can do another 20 requests at 11:02:05. Figure 6-10 illustrates how the fixed-window counter algorithm can allow six requests to succeed between the 1.5-minute and 2.5-minute window marks, when the defined rate limit is four requests per minute.

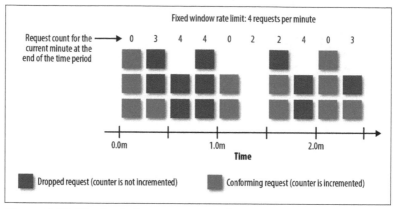

Figure 6-10. Fixed-window counter rate-limiting in practice

If your API can tolerate these kinds of bursts, the fixed-window counter algorithm could be suitable for you. API providers like Twitter use this algorithm.

Sliding-window counter

As the name suggests, the sliding-window counter algorithm allows you to keep track of traffic in a sliding window of time, ensuring that the API can reject the "bursty" traffic that's possible with the token bucket and fixed-window counter algorithm.

To implement the sliding-window algorithm, just incrementing a single counter is not enough. Instead, we divide the rate-limit window into individual buckets of time. For example, to implement a 20 requests/minute rate limit, we might divide a 1-minute window into 60 buckets and maintain a counter for each second. These buckets can simply expire after one minute. On each request, we sum up the counters recorded in the last minute. If the total exceeds the rate limit, we reject the request. If you want to implement a lenient sliding window, you can sum the last 59 buckets before deciding whether the current request should be accepted. Figure 6-11 shows how the sliding-window counter algorithm can reject bursty traffic in practice.

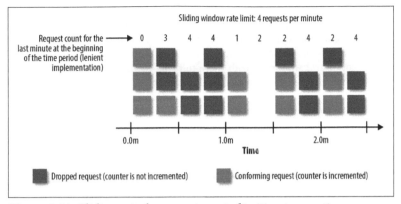

Figure 6-11. Sliding-window counter rate-limiting in practice

Instagram uses the sliding-window counter algorithm to rate-limit its API. If you want to ensure that traffic to your API remains steady from each developer, the sliding-window counter could be suitable for you.

Pro Tip

Before launching a new rate-limiting policy or algorithm, *dark launch* it to understand how much and which traffic it will block. To do that, use logging to analyze how many requests would be rejected, without actually rejecting any requests. You might want to adjust your thresholds as you learn about the impact they will have.

Expert Advice

All Uber developers must create an account and register with us. Developers can automatically create production calls against their own accounts (i.e., request a real Uber to come pick them up) and other registered developer accounts, but they must request extended permissions to make calls on behalf of other users. Each developer is automatically rate-limited, and we recommend that developers reach out to explain clearly and transparently why they might need additional API quota. In some cases, we would see a spike in traffic in one of our developer's API keys, and we'd reach out to find out what was going on. Depending on the nature and volume of the traffic, we might not throttle them right away, pending more information.

We also presented our developer terms of service in plain language and enforced them through legal means when we found developers violated them. Oftentimes, we simply reached out to the developer and let them know that their use of the API wasn't cool—and we'd work with them to bring them into compliance. In other cases, the developer didn't care about the terms and kept abusing their access even after warnings made in consultation with Uber Legal; in those rare and unfortunate cases, we revoked their API access.

—Chris Messina, developer experience lead at Uber

Rate Limits and Developers

Rate limits are among the things that developers hate. Often, rate limits force developers to write additional code or just confuse them about why their requests are being rejected. If you implement a rate-limiting system, you might like to do a few additional things to make developers' lives easier. Let's take a look at these.

Return appropriate HTTP status codes

When developers hit your rate limit, deny the request by returning an HTTP 429 status code, as shown in Example 6-2, which indicates that the user has sent too many requests in a given amount of time. It's also standard to set the `retry-after` header to let developers programmatically retry the request.

Example 6-2. Slack API returning 429 and retry-after header when the rate limit is reached

```
$ curl -I https://slack.com/api/rtm.connect
HTTP/2 429
Date: Sun, 17 Jun 2018 14:43:38 GMT
retry-after: 36
```

Rate-limit custom response headers

Along with the status code, you should include custom response headers explaining the rate limit. These headers will help developers decide programmatically when they should retry the API call. Here are a few commonly used custom headers:

`X-RateLimit-Limit`
> The maximum rate at which a developer can call this endpoint in a given amount of time.

`X-RateLimit-Remaining`
> The number of requests that are available to the developer in the current interval. If you're using the token bucket algorithm, this can indicate the number of tokens remaining in the applicable bucket.

`X-RateLimit-Reset`
> The time at which the current rate-limit window resets in UTC epoch seconds.

Example 6-3 depicts example rate-limit headers as seen from a GitHub API call.

Example 6-3. GitHub API returning rate-limit headers when the rate limit is reached

```
$ curl -I https://api.github.com/users/saurabhsahni

HTTP/1.1 200 OK
Date: Sat, 11 Nov 2017 04:37:22 GMT
Status: 200 OK
X-RateLimit-Limit: 60
X-RateLimit-Remaining: 59
X-RateLimit-Reset: 1510378642
```

Rate-limit status API

If you have different rate limits for different API endpoints, your developers might like to have an API that they can call to query the rate-limit status across various API endpoints. This way, they can programmatically keep track of available requests per endpoint.

Documenting rate limits

Developers need to mind their rate-limit constraints when using an API. By documenting your rate-limit values, you will help your developers in making the right architectural choices. Most of the popular APIs clearly document rate limits. This way, developers can learn about them before actually running into rate-limit errors. Apart from rate-limit values, you should also consider documenting best practices that developers can follow to avoid hitting the rate limit.

Expert Advice

The GitHub REST API has a flat 5,000 authenticated calls per hour rate limit, but those calls could come all at once. We saw this happen a variety of times when a Chrome extension or an integrator's script went a little haywire. At a certain scale, rate limits based on authenticated users can only be one small part of an overall system meant to protect your application. We now have per-service rate limits to avoid saturation, content creation back-offs to avoid creating too many issues in a short period of time, and other abuse protections to avoid answering exponentially more API requests within a window of a few seconds.

If we were to redo the rate-limiting, we'd likely choose a smaller rate-limit window similar to folks like Twitter: you get 250 calls every 10 minutes.

—Kyle Daigle, director of ecosystem engineering at GitHub

Rate-Limiting Best Practices

Here are a few best practices to like to consider when adding rate-limiting to an API:

- Pick the rate-limiting algorithm based on the traffic pattern that you want to support. Generally, paid services are lenient with traffic bursts and choose the token bucket algorithm. Others choose a fixed window or sliding window.

- Choose rate-limit thresholds such that common API use cases are not rate-limited.

- Provide clear guidance to external developers on what your rate-limit thresholds are and how can they request additional quota.

- Before granting additional quota to a developer, you might want to understand why they need to exceed the rate limits, what their use case is, and what the current usage pattern is. If your infrastructure can support additional quota and there is no better way to achieve the same result, you might want to consider giving them an exception.

- Starting with lower rate-limit thresholds is helpful. Increasing rate-limit thresholds is easier than reducing them because reducing them can negatively affect active developer apps.
- Implement exponential back-off in your client SDKs and provide sample code to developers on how to do that. This way, developers are less likely to continue hitting your API when they are rate-limited. For more information, see "Error Handling and Exponential Back-Off" on page 115.
- Use rate limits to reduce the impact of incidents by heavily rate-limiting noncritical traffic during an outage.

Lessons Learned from Slack's Rate-Limiting

In March 2018, Slack rolled out an evolved rate-limiting system. Until then, the rate limits for Slack API methods were quite vague and often unenforced. In the absence of documented rate limits, developers building applications using the Slack API often assumed that they would not be rate-limited. However, sometimes that assumption backfired when their applications were installed by large enterprise customers.

To introduce new rate-limit thresholds, Slack analyzed use cases for each API and defined thresholds ensuring that most common use cases could be accomplished by applications without getting rate-limited. Before launching new rate-limit thresholds, the team launched dark tests to figure out which applications would get rate-limited in the new system. While in some cases Slack adjusted its rate-limit thresholds, in other cases it was clear that the developer's implementation was not efficient.

The Slack team could have launched the new rate-limit thresholds without any warning. However, the team members figured that it would be a breaking change for those developers that might now get rate-limited due to the new thresholds. To ensure the best experience for these developers and for customers, they granted a brief grace period to those apps to adjust their implementations. The new documented rate limits helped developers in making better architectural decisions while building their app and mitigated rate-limit surprises in production.

—Saurabh Sahni, staff engineer at Slack

Developer SDKs

A *developer software development kit* (SDK) is a set of tools that allow developers to create applications on a specific platform. By providing SDKs, you are not just simplifying the integration effort required, you are also helping developers follow the best practices for working with your API. When developers are able to follow best practices, that will in turn create more optimal usage patterns for your API, which will help you scale.

 For more general information on SDKs, see Chapter 9.

The following sections describe a few things that you should consider when creating an SDK to help with scaling of your API.

Rate-Limiting Support

Developers do not want to write additional code to work with your rate limits. So, if you provide SDKs, you should ensure that they work well with your rate limits. Your SDK code should parse the rate-limit headers returned in API responses and slow down the request rate, if necessary. Your SDK should also gracefully handle 429 errors and retry only after the time indicated by the rate-limit headers.

Pagination Support

Retrieving results that spread across pages is often difficult. It's especially easy to hit rate limits when requesting multiple pages in a loop. By adding support for working with your paginated APIs, you can ensure that rate limits and errors are gracefully handled. At the same time, you probably want to support some upper limit on how many pages to fetch.

Using gzip

Using gzip compression in your SDKs is a simple and effective way to reduce the bandwidth needed for each API call. Although compressing and decompressing content consumes additional CPU resources, this is often a great trade-off for reducing network costs.

Caching Frequently Used Data

You can add support for storing API responses or frequently used data locally in a cache. This can help in reducing the number of API calls you will receive. If you have concerns or policies around what data clients can store, ensuring that the cache automatically expires in a few hours can help.

Error Handling and Exponential Back-Off

Errors are often handled poorly by developers. It's difficult for developers to reproduce all possible errors during development, and that's why they might not write code to handle those errors gracefully.

As you build your SDK, first, you could implement local checks to return errors on invalid requests. For example, your SDK can reject an API call locally if it's missing a required parameter for an API method. This way, you can often prevent invalid API requests from hitting your servers.

You should also build support for the actions the client application should take when a request fails. Some failures, like authorization errors, cannot be addressed by a retry. Your SDK should surface appropriate errors for these failures to the developer. For other errors, it's simply better for the SDK to automatically retry the API call.

To help developers avoid making too many API calls to your server, your SDK should implement *exponential back-off*. This is a standard error-handling strategy in which client applications periodically retry a failed request over an increasing amount of time. Exponential back-off can help in reducing the number of requests your server receives. When your SDKs implement this, it helps your web application recover gracefully from outages.

SDK Best Practices

Here are some best practices for building SDKs that will help you with scaling your API:

- Stability, security, and reliability for SDKs are critical. Any bug in an SDK might require updates from several developers. Depending on how many developers are using your SDK, even a simple upgrade can be quite difficult. Thoroughly testing your SDK before releasing is highly recommended.

- If you're building a mobile SDK, you need to further optimize size, memory usage, CPU usage, network interactions, and battery performance.

- Implementing complex API operations like OAuth in your SDKs helps to speed up the onboarding experience for your developers.

- Handle rate limits and errors gracefully. Build protections into your SDK to avoid too many concurrent calls to your API servers.

- Make troubleshooting easy by surfacing errors to developers and allowing them to turn on logging.

- The way you package your SDK affects adoption. Use appropriate platforms, like npm, CocoaPods, RubyGems, or pip, to distribute your SDKs.

Closing Thoughts

Scaling an API is not just about supporting more requests per second. There are other creative ways to support growing numbers of customers. It's important to understand what scalability issues you're running into and why. Do your developers actually need to make the number of API calls they are making? Would changes to your API design help in reducing that volume? Can developers use your API more efficiently? Answering these questions, along with feedback from your developers, will help you be more successful in scaling your API.

As you refine your API design, policies, and tools, these changes can sometimes affect your developers. In Chapter 7, you learn how to release these changes while keeping your developers informed.

Managing Change

Good design is never frozen in time. Just because you made a great design today does not mean that it will continue to be good when change is afoot. Good APIs need to be able to adapt and change along with the evolution of your product or business.

Breaking changes are one of the common pitfalls of many APIs. In this chapter, we discuss how to approach change with an eye for consistency as well as how to ensure backward compatibility as your API evolves.

Expert Advice

An API should be consistent, clear, and well documented. Small inconsistencies around things like naming and URLs add up to a lot of confusion as your API ages. Because you want to keep from making breaking changes, you want to do your best to remain consistent but more importantly ensure that new additions are clear and obvious for integrators.

—Kyle Daigle, director of ecosystem engineering at GitHub

Toward Consistency

Consistency is the hallmark of excellent experiences of any kind— APIs are no exception. Consistency builds trust. Trust is the foundation to creating a thriving developer ecosystem.

Here are some of the hallmarks of consistency:

- Developers are able to build a mental model of how to access data in your system.
- Response objects are formulated with strict types and meaningful names; that is, each model is the same regardless of the endpoint.
- Developers can use the same request patterns across a number of endpoints, which reduces the need for middleware and helps applications perform and scale.
- Requests fail predictably with meaningful errors.

Sometimes, despite our best intentions, APIs can become inconsistent. Take Slack's API, for example. API endpoints had been added incrementally over time without any central design oversight. Each product group within the company designed and released API methods independently. As a result, inconsistencies emerged. Table 7-1 shows simplified request patterns for two similar API methods, channels.join and channels.invite.

Table 7-1. Simplified requests for two Slack API methods in 2017: channels.join and channels.invite

Takes a channel name	Takes a channel ID

`// Join a channel`
`channels.join({`
`  channel: "channel-name"`
`})`
	`// Invite a user to a channel`
	`channels.invite({`
	`  channel: "C12345",`
	`  user: "U23456"`
	`})`

In Table 7-1, you can see how one endpoint takes a channel as a string name, whereas the other takes a channel as an ID. This type of inconsistency hurts developers, because for a developer to be able to use both of these endpoints, they now need to store both the channel ID and channel name and to create a layer of logic to determine which one to use to assemble a request. What if the channel name changes? The developer is additionally responsible for keeping the channel name up to date.

Consistency might sound simple enough, and it's easy to create a consistent experience if you have the opportunity to design everything at once with no historical constraints. But after you have active developers using your API, things become complicated. As companies and products evolve, new changes to the API can seem like a constant negotiation between consistency with the past and correctness for the future.

Let's look at a fictitious example to illustrate what might happen. Suppose Company A has released new API with one method that lets a developer fetch all of a user's repositories at once. Initially, the product allowed for only 10 repositories per user. Example 7-1 presents a response payload for an original API method from the initial API offering, `repositories.fetch`.

Example 7-1. Response payload for repositories.fetch

```
{
  "repositories": [
    {
      "id": 12345
    },
    {
      "id": 23456
    }
  ]
}
```

After a few months, the company has grown. It adds a new price tier to the product that enables unlimited repositories per user. A year later, a number of power users have accumulated millions of repositories. Company B has built a popular application that uses `repositories.fetch`. Although the number of repositories has expanded, the `repositories.fetch` endpoint has continued to lack a pagination mechanism. (For more information on pagination, see Chapter 4.) Now, API requests to `repositories.fetch` are timing out because the repositories must be aggregated across multiple database shards.

As a result of a weekend service outage that was caused by too many calls to `repositories.fetch`, Company A has agreed with Company B to release a new endpoint that returns a single repository, `repositories.fetchSingle`, which you can see in Example 7-2.

Example 7-2. Response payload for repositories.fetchSingle

```
[
  {
    "12345": {...}
```

```
    }
]
```

Now Company A has two endpoints, shown side by side in Table 7-2 for easy comparison.

Table 7-2. Side-by-side comparison of repositories.fetch and repositories.fetchSingle payloads

Endpoint 1	Endpoint 2
`repositories.fetch()`	`repositories.fetchSingle(12345)`

```
repositories.fetch()    repositories.fetchSingle(12345)
{                       [
  "repositories": [       {
    {                       "12345": {...}
      "id": 12345         }
    },                  ]
    {
      "id": 23456
    }
  ]
}
```

Notice the inconsistencies when comparing the payloads for these two very similar endpoints. For `repositories.fetch` the response includes a key (`"repositories"`) whose value is an array of objects containing IDs keyed by `"id"`.

In contrast, `repositories.fetchSingle` returns an array without the `"repositories"` key. Inside of that array is an array of objects keyed by the actual ID value, instead of by the string `"id"`.

Although this is a fictitious story, it's not an uncommon pattern at growing companies. After the initial version of an API is released, additional changes might be made that are inconsistent. Developers adopt these new features, along with their inconsistencies. That is how inconsistency develops—and sticks—as an API evolves. Luckily, to help prevent these types of inconsistencies, there are technological tools and organizational processes, and we cover some of them in the following sections.

Automated Testing

It's important that everyone who impacts the API understands and supports consistency, but it's difficult to enforce as an organizational value. And you cannot expect people to always make the right decisions for the system, especially when they need to reconsider the minutiae of a complex system for every decision. That's where automated testing comes into play.

Continuous integration (CI) is the practice of merging all developers' working copies to a single shared repository, often multiple times a day. The workflow in which a code change goes from being written to approved and merged is called a *CI pipeline* (Figure 7-1). Adding an automated testing step (see Step 3 in Figure 7-1) before developers are allowed to merge their code is a great choice for preventing unwanted changes from sneaking into the API—especially the backward incompatible ones. These test suites are useful for catching regressions as you develop your API.

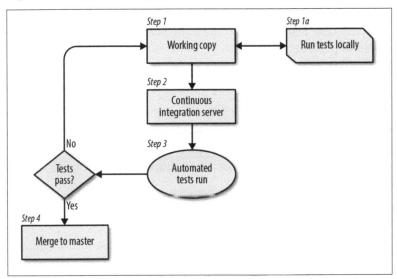

Figure 7-1. A CI pipeline

When you're implementing an automated test suite, it must give internal developers timely feedback, minimize false positives, and empower internal developers to make the right choices in their API design. The tests themselves should validate input, expected behavior, and the correct data types in the response payload. The more individuals there are who are empowered to write high-quality automation tests, the more useful your CI pipeline will be in ensuring data reliability for your APIs.

You might also choose to include additional approval requirements in the CI pipeline prior to code merge for any changes that affect the output of the API. After changes that affect the API are detected, the code change can be automatically submitted for specific people to review before it can be merged. Those reviewers could have a process for making sure that requests and responses are consistent with the APIs that are already released.

Automated testing should be a part of your internal development life cycle; it brings high visibility and responsiveness to code changes. The more you can catch unwanted changes before they occur, the better off you are.

If you don't have CI, run automated tests continuously off the code mainline to measure the health of your API. Run the tests as frequently as possible to begin with. Then, as you build your CI pipeline, make them nonblocking and monitor the results. When you have 0% false negatives, turn them on as blocking tests, so that failures will prevent merges.

In summary, you need to craft a process to ensure that internal developers get timely feedback on design decisions and proposed changes before they merge code.

In addition to having your CI pipeline ensure backward compatibility, there are additional mechanisms that can help ensure consistency for APIs, which we discuss in more detail in the subsections that follow.

API description languages

In service-oriented architecture, you would be able to use an interface description language (IDL) to define requests and a type system to validate responses. However, there is no advantage to using these tools for external-facing APIs, because you have no control over the requesters' behavior. Because of that, you need to take a different approach to defining the interfaces of your API.

JavaScript Object Notation (JSON) is a widely used format that is both flexible and expressive, and it's the format for all the API examples in this book. As JSON becomes more rich and expressive, it cannot be constrained to the same type systems that most programming languages have. As a result, if you are providing a JSON web API, you need to think carefully about the tools you use to manage changes for both responses and requests.

First, let's talk about describing and validating responses.

Describing and validating responses

The first thing you want to validate with automated tests is response payloads. Luckily, you don't need to write this validation from scratch.

There are tools that help you to describe the interface of an API in a structured way that can be used to generate documentation and run your tests. Additionally, a subset of these tools also allows you to specify data types and custom data types. Some examples (*https://en.wikipedia.org/wiki/Overview_of_RESTful_API_Descrip tion_Languages*) are json:api, JSON Schema, and Apache Avro.

The code examples that follow include samples of a simple JSON Schema system and a corresponding test using the RSpec library for Ruby. These examples illustrate validation for a simple and flat JSON response—yours might end up being much more complicated. These are intended to give a high-level understanding of how JSON validation can happen in your CI pipeline.

Example 7-3 shows the definition of the payload response for `repo sitories.fetch`. There are many more features to the JSON Schema than are shown here. As a basic example, this schema illustrates that all fields are required and that there are no additional optional fields with `"additionalProperties": false`. It also lists a single required field in the response, keyed as `"repositories"`. In the `"properties"` object, each required field is described with `"type": "array"` and points to a single definition of what each item in the array should look like.

Example 7-3. JSON Schema definition

```
{
  "$schema": "http://json-schema.org/draft-04/schema#",
  "title": "repositories.fetch",
  "description": "Schema for repositories.fetch response payload",
  "type": "object",
  "additionalProperties": false,
  "required": [
    "repositories"
  ],
  "properties": {
    "repositories": {
      "type": "array",
      "items": {
        "$ref": "../common_objects_schema.json#/repository"
```

```
        }
      }
    }
  }
}
```

Example 7-4 is a definition of the repository that was referenced in Example 7-3 as `"../common_objects_schema.json#/repository"`. This particular object will have required fields, each with its own corresponding unique properties. This object definition is a powerful building block in maintaining consistency in your API. These are reusable objects that can be consumed in a variety of JSON Schemas for other endpoints. The stricter these reusable object definitions are and the more they're used throughout the other JSON Schema definitions, the more you can guarantee that your responses have similar payloads when describing the same object type.

Example 7-4. A JSON Schema definition for a single "repository" that can be reused in a number of other JSON Schema specifications

```json
{
  "$schema": "http://json-schema.org/draft-04/schema#",
  "repository": {
    "type": "object",
    "additionalProperties": false,
    "required": [
      "id",
      "name",
      "description",
      "created"
    ],
    "properties": {
      "id": {
        "type": "integer"
      },
      "name": {
        "type": "string"
      },
      "description": {
        "type": "string"
      },
      "created": {
        "type": "integer"
      }
    }
  }
}
```

In Example 7-5, you can see an example RSpec test that calls the API endpoint and then uses a helper to validate the response against the JSON Schema. You can run the RSpec tests (or whatever you choose for your automated tests) on demand or as part of a CI system. You should update the JSON Schema—or however you choose to define your response payloads—every time the response payload changes.

Example 7-5. RSpec test using JSON Schema definition

```
describe 'repositories.fetch' do
  # fetch all repositories
  ...
  it "can fetch all repositories successfully", acceptance: true do
    create_repository_factory (product: 'std')

    step "call repositories.fetch endpoint"
    response = @client.repositories.fetch().response_body

    step 'Validate API response and its schema for "ok: true"'
    expect (response).to_match_json_schema(repositories.fetch)
  end
  end
  end
end
```

Describing and validating requests

Now that you've seen how to validate API response payloads, what about requests? Because you can't control how developers use the API, your best bet is to define a clear interface that creates flexibility while guiding developers toward the best choices and patterns. Additionally, a good request definition interface also allows for you to define reusable types, just like the reusable object definitions in the JSON Schema in Example 7-4.

Thankfully, there are tools to help you define your request structure so that you don't need to build it from scratch. Just like for API responses, you can use JSON Schema to describe and validate API requests, as long as the request is in JSON or you can reliably transform it to JSON. Additionally, tools like Swagger use a different specification called OpenAPI, formerly known as the Swagger Specification, to describe REST APIs. Your API does not necessarily need to be RESTful to get a huge benefit out of this system—the only requirement is that you use the web. Swagger also has a mechanism to automatically generate documentation. Similarly, OpenAPI enables code generation for libraries and SDKs.

Regardless of whether you use JSON Schema or OpenAPI, implementing a request specification system can have many uses. In addition to documentation, this system can also do some error checking and validation of inbound API requests. When your request fields have strict types, you can send an error if the request is poorly formatted. This saves you the effort of assembling a bad response payload, and it provides better feedback to the developer.

The lack of ability to control third-party API requests means that mistakes will be born out of an assumption that you and your users are like-minded. Don't forget that human creativity is limitless, and users will use your API in ways you never imagined.

That's why documentation is key. When you create a request specification and integrate it closely with your documentation, you help developers make the right choices. In your documentation, you need to communicate the state of the world today, along with a history of significant changes you might have made in the past. You might also need to carve out a space to describe forthcoming changes.

Storytime: API Metadata at Slack

When Dan Bornstein started working as a software engineer on the Developer Platform team at Slack, there was no standard definition of API requests, despite the API rapidly developing a large following. So Dan created the API metadata system to describe requests for every API method. Initially, the system catalogued request parameters that were being used based on historic traffic. As soon as the initial system was put in place using historic traffic, the API metadata became a proactive way for Slack's software engineers to describe API interfaces. API metadata was used to generate documentation, even going so far as to turn request fields into an interactive API tester. API metadata was also plugged into the data warehouse so that analytics reports could be pulled on API traffic. Eventually, it grew to be a layer in between the web request and response fulfillment. This layer handled argument validation, generic errors and warnings, token type validation, and more. It became an extensible way to catch early exceptions in requests before going through the effort of assembling a response.

Backward Compatibility

If you're using a query system like GraphQL, where requests must specify the desired fields, you might have a good idea of which fields are actively being used. But if your API is anything like the vast majority of third-party APIs in the wild, you most likely return all the relevant fields in your JSON payloads. And even if you were using a *QL framework, there's always the possibility that developers will select all fields. In both of these cases, you have no visibility into which fields are being used—you know only that they're all being requested.

For certain companies and products, backward compatibility is non-negotiable. At Cloudinary, the API maintains total backward compatibility because image URLs based on the API are everywhere. Luckily, they designed the interfaces to be extensible and future-proof, making the main challenge that of educating customers about new features and additions.

Backward compatibility is a huge consideration for anybody developing an API, especially for API providers who have external users. It's somewhat easier to negotiate and change an API response when the dependencies are within a company than when the dependencies are external.

Storytime: Slack's Missing Field

In March 2016, Slack did not yet have an API metadata system. It did not have JSON Schema or RSpec tests. The Slack platform had only just officially launched three months prior.

An inconsistent API request had been out in the wild, to the chagrin of Slack native mobile clients. Third-party bots could call chat.postMessage with the as_user parameter. When false, the message posted would have a flag, is_bot=true. With as_user=true, the is_bot flag was missing, and bot-impersonated messages were indistinguishable from actual user messages.

Slack wanted impersonation to be allowed, but in a way that was clear to human users that the messages had come from a bot. The solution was to always set the is_bot field on all message payloads. The decision was toward consistency—the field would always be set, regardless of whether the value was true or false. Slack developers decided to fix the problem once and for all and quietly update that undocumented field to always be there.

Ordinarily, setting a field consistently is a virtue.

But one of the most popular apps in the ecosystem had taken advantage of this idiosyncratic field setting. Instead of checking the value, the app checked for the presence of the key for its business logic. It relied on this inconsistency for its app. When the change was made to set the is_bot field no matter what, the app broke. One of Slack's most widely used apps suddenly became unavailable due to a functionality change in Slack's API:

```
WARNING:
Developer reporting an outage due to change in
chat.postMessage parameter as_user.
```

What was supposed to be a fix became an error. Slack ended up rolling back the change, giving developers three months to find a way around it. On April 13, Slack published a blog post (*https:// medium.com/slack-developer-blog/api-update-new-field-in-api- responses-d23076ea2ef3*) announcing the change. The change to make the field consistent went live again on April 30.

The lesson here is that even if you get things wrong in your API, you need to think carefully about how you will roll out a fix to minimize impact to developers. Think beyond your expectations of how developers will use your API. You can't always predict what others will build with your API—and you cannot control how they decide to implement their apps.

Planning for and Communicating Change

Many technical design resources can help you craft your design for a greenfield project. But if your API is successful, you'll be working for years in a nongreenfield area. This means that you and your developers will be interfacing with your past decisions for a long time, and all new design decisions will carry context from before.

You need to decide how tolerant your system should be of different types of changes. In addition to that, you should develop a robust communication system with your API users. Think about the types of changes you will make, the impact of those changes on developers, and what the appropriate communication should be. This can take some time and practice to refine, but having a communication plan is key.

Communication Plan

When it comes to creating a communication plan, ensure that developers have a mechanism to receive updates. A rich site summary (RSS) feed is a good start, but eventually you'll also want a way to communicate with specific developers about changes that affect them.

Using our previous example of using `repositories.fetch` and `repositories.fetchSingle`, you might want to contact all of the developers who used the `repositories.fetch` endpoint in the past 12 months in order to provide them with updates about the brand-new `repositories.fetchSingle` endpoint. You might even want to contact all developers who used the `repositories.fetch` endpoint and received a 500-level response after you released the product that caused timeouts.

Table 7-3 shows possible communication channels and timelines for backward-compatible and backward-incompatible changes. In this particular example, backward-compatible changes can be released at any time, and developers will be given 18 months' notice before backward incompatible changes are released.

Table 7-3. Example categories of types of changes

	Backward compatible	Backward incompatible
Examples	Request parameter added, response field added, new API method added	Response field removed, functionality changes, response type changes, endpoint removed
Communication channel	RSS feed API docs	RSS feed API docs Email to affected developers Blog post explaining change
Time to release after notification	Anytime	18 months

In addition to communication mechanisms, in which you broadcast information to specific audiences, there are other built-in ways to communicate. You might consider annotating response payloads or headers with information about changes. Example 7-6 shows how that might look in the payload of the `repositories.fetch` endpoint.

Example 7-6. Adding response metadata to communicate with developers

```
// GET repositories.fetch()

{
  "repositories": [
    {
      "id": 12345
    },
    {
      "id": 23456
    }
  ],
  "response_metadata":{
    "response_change": {
            "date": "January 1, 2021",
            "severity": 1,
            "affected_object": "repository",
            "details": "Starting January 1, 2021, a new field `date`
                        will be added to each repository object"
        }
  }
}
```

Your communication plan needs to strike a balance between giving developers appropriate notice for changes and allowing your API to evolve. If you're making a lot of changes, the overhead of communication grows proportionally to the amount of process you add. Think about where you can automate your communication alongside your code releases to reduce the overhead of customizing each communication channel.

Expert Advice

We definitely keep the lines of communication open when managing change. We're very proactive in ensuring our developers know what to expect. We do a lot through our channels—blog posts, emails, and other outreach. We understand how important this is.

—Desiree Motamedi Ward, head of developer product marketing at Facebook

---

Adding

Of all the changes you can make to your API, additions are the easiest. Whether you're adding a new endpoint or a new field, these changes are often simple to execute, if done correctly.

In the case of adding response fields, adding a new JSON key–value pair is almost always backward compatible and won't affect developers. This is especially true if your fields are always consistently set, regardless of their value. (Consistently typed fields will be useful for generating code, which some API providers do to create their SDKs.) The same applies for query-based interfaces: adding a "column" is easier than removing one.

Even though adding response fields is more straightforward than removing them, there are still a few things to consider for backward compatibility:

Was the field set before?
> If the field wasn't set before but you've decided to set it consistently, ask yourself whether a developer could be relying on the fact that the field is unset.

Will everyone want the new field?
> Sometimes, you need to provide a mechanism for developers to opt in to the new field(s). In this case, you might consider a new endpoint or a new request parameter.
>
> Adding new request parameters to control output may seem like an easy choice. However, use this option with caution. When you add too many request parameters, your API endpoint becomes significantly harder to describe with tools like JSON Schema. Therefore, it becomes more and more difficult to test with automated tools.
>
> Adding new endpoints can also seem like an attractive choice to enable new features. However, you want to make sure that your new endpoints are consistent with your previous ones, that developers have a seamless upgrade path (do their existing authorizations work with the new endpoint?), and that you aren't overcrowding your namespace with a limited feature.

Removing

Given that you need to continue to evolve your API, there will be endpoints and fields that you may want to deprecate completely. So, let's look at how you can ease the transition for developers. These types of changes require significant communication and infrastructure overhead.

Expert Advice

Don't overcomplicate your API and don't future-proof it too much. Often by future-proofing your API, you make it too generic and/or too complex. Developers building applications on (or using) your platform are building stuff for the "now." They like to move quickly and are not always thinking 10 steps ahead. Your API should cater to this mindset.

—Yochay Kiriaty, Azure principal program manager at Microsoft

---

When taking something away from developers, you need to ease the transition with a carrot, an incentive to get them to switch to something new. What features are you enabling? Is there a problem that you couldn't fix with the deprecated endpoint that you're fixing in some other way? These are things you should be clear about before you make your deprecation announcement. Sometimes, you may need to make the new feature especially enticing to developers by also packaging it with an end-user feature.

Storytime: Slack's Conversations API

As Slack rapidly launched features from 2015 to 2016, API methods to retrieve channels became increasingly complicated and difficult to maintain. The engineering teams reached a critical inflection point in 2017, with the launch of Shared Channels. As a result, they released Shared Channels through a new suite of API methods: the Conversations API. They made it easy to switch to the new system, and they incentivized developers by offering data exclusively through the new API methods.

As part of easing the transition, you *definitely* want to communicate with developers about the fields that are being deprecated. After you've started your communication, give developers adequate time to stop using the deprecated fields or endpoints.

A deprecation timeline that's too short can erode trust with your developers and stymie the adoption of your API. Companies often implement policies establishing the minimum length of time that they will support API releases. For example, as of this writing, Salesforce commits to supporting each API version for a minimum of three years from the date of first release. Before deprecating an API version, Salesforce gives at least one year's notice directly to customers.

Some API specifications have standards for how to handle deprecation. GraphQL offers the ability to mark certain fields as deprecated. The specification states:

> 3.1.2.2 Object Field deprecation
>
> Fields in an object may be marked as deprecated as deemed necessary by the application. It is still legal to query for these fields (to ensure existing clients are not broken by the change), but the fields should be appropriately treated in documentation and tooling.
>
> —From the GraphQL spec, working draft, October 2016

Versioning

As we mentioned in Chapter 4, to bundle changes into understandable chunks and to give developers a way to understand your API, you might want to consider versioning. The following sections describe a few possible strategies for handling versioning.

Additive-change strategy

In an additive-change strategy, all updates are compatible with previous versions. The following changes are considered backward incompatible and should be avoided when using the additive-change strategy:

- Removing or renaming APIs or API parameters
- Changing a type for a response field
- Changes in behavior for an existing API
- Changes in error codes and fault contracts

In this strategy, you make changes, such as adding an output field or adding a new API endpoint. However, you never want to change a response field's type or remove a response field without letting users opt in via request parameters. This means that in order to do this, you'll add more and more parameters that will alter the response of an API request. Table 7-4 illustrates how that would look for a fictitious REST API to retrieve a user resource.

Table 7-4. Requests and responses for a REST API

Example request opting out of friends list	Example request default payload
`GET /users/1234?exclude_friends=1`	`GET /users/1234`

```
{
    "id": 1234,
    "name":"Chen Hong",
    "username:" "chenhong",
    "date_joined": 1514773798
}
```

```
{
    "id": 1234,
    "name":"Chen Hong",
    "username:""chenhong",
    "date_joined": 1514773798,
    "friends": [
        2341,
        3449,
        2352,
        2353,
        2358
    ]
}
```

In the example in Table 7-4, `exclude_friends` is an added request parameter that changes the response payload.

With clear rules, there isn't too much process that needs to be hashed out within the organization.

Explicit-version strategy

The first thing you need to decide when you create an explicitly numbered versioning system is how users will interact with versions. This is often called a versioning *scheme*. There are a few choices available, which we look at here. Each one has distinct advantages. Ultimately, the version access pattern should be as stable as promised in accompanying documentation, and developers should have the option to opt into new versions while maintaining stability on previous versions.

Updating *URI components* is one strategy that many API providers use to define version schemes. These are often inserted as a base for the URI, before the specification of a resource-like entity. For example, take Uber's ride requests API endpoint, `https://api.uber.c om/v1.2/requests`. In this example, `v1.2` is inserted before the *requests* resource. This is similar to the scheme for Twitter's Ads API, in which `2` is the version: `https:/ /ads-api.twitter.c om/2/accounts`. An alternative to including the version before the resource is placing the version *after* the resource, which would imply that the version is specific to the resource or API method rather than the entire suite of API methods.

The benefit of specifying versions in URI components is that many programming languages, libraries, and SDKs have support for easily binding a request to a version using a base URI. Additionally, if the bulk of requests are `GET` requests, depending on your authorization system, it's easy for developers to debug and inspect endpoints with the browser. This scheme should *not* be used, however, if you're not ready to support these endpoints as permalinks, because the pattern implies a certain level of resource permanence in the REST paradigm. Finally, if you elect to use URI components to version your API, be prepared to support 300-level HTTP status codes to indicate redirection for moved or moving resources.

Using *HTTP headers* is another way to specify versions. You can do this through custom headers, such as Stripe's `Stripe-Version` header, or through the `Accept/Content-Type` header (`Accept: application/json; version=1`) or through the `Accept` header with a custom media type (`Accept: application/custom_media +type.api.v1 + json`). This scheme is less visible than a URI component, which can make it less desirable for experimentation in the browser, and it can have implications regarding client caching if the client interprets two requests to different versions as the same request. It can, however, reduce URI bloat.

The final option is using *request parameters*. In this scheme, you allow users to request versions alongside any other request parameters. Here's an example request from the Google Maps API: *https:// maps.googleapis.com/maps/api/js?v=3*. The *v=3* inserted in the query string is used to select the version number. This has similar benefits as versioning with URI components, but depending on your application stack, it can be more difficult to route these requests because of the high variability of query parameters and their types, as well as the fact that query parameters are resolved after the URI.

Of course, there's more to versioning than the mechanics of how your users will specify version numbers. Behind the scenes, there are many more decisions for you to make for your code base. For instance, how will you ensure backward compatibility for old versions? Developers might be building businesses that rely on the stability of your API, and, as we mentioned before, they might not retire old versions for years. In many cases, maintaining these many versions results in forked code bases or code paths, where new functions will be created that call into old functions, as demonstrated in Figure 7-2.

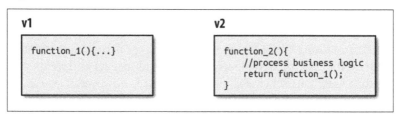

Figure 7-2. Diagram of versioned function names

Alternatively, you might be forking your code path such that requests route to a new controller responsible for executing them, as shown in Figure 7-3.

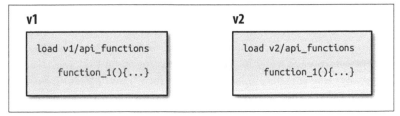

v1	v2
load v1/api_functions	load v2/api_functions
function_1(){...}	function_1(){...}

Figure 7-3. Diagram of versioned controller

Finally, another way to maintain versions in your code base is to create transformations between each version (Figure 7-4). In this case, there is a main function that is updated, and that function has various transformation functions corresponding to the schemas of previous versions. The transformation functions convert the data to the appropriate schema before returning the data.

```
v1, v2

function_1(){
    // assemble data
    $output_data = []

    if (v1) {
        $output_data = transform_v1($output_data)
    }

    return $output_data
}
```

Figure 7-4. Pseudocode sample of a transformation layer between version 2 and version 1

In addition to implementing the versioning system, you and your team need to think about how to organize and label your versions. For this, the semantic versioning specification (SemVer) can be helpful in using a standard to describe your changes. In SemVer, there are MAJOR, MINOR, and PATCH versions (in the format MAJOR.MINOR.PATCH). MAJOR versions are for backward-incompatible API changes. MINOR versions are for adding functionality in a backward-compatible manner. PATCH versions are for backward-compatible bug fixes.

The convention for documenting major changes is a whole number jump, such as *v1* to *v2*. The convention for minor and patch changes is incrementing decimal places after the number, such as *v1.1* to *v1.2* or *v1.1.0* to *v1.1.1*. Even when using SemVer, you need to decide how granularly to version requests and what types of changes are acceptable in each version. For example, you might decide to automatically roll all developers forward into new MINOR version bumps, because those are backward-compatible changes. Another strategy could be to apply all minor changes to previous versions without any named version bump. A new response field might appear in both *v2* and *v1*.

Table 7-5 presents an example chart that a company might use to provide a framework for major and minor change versioning.

Table 7-5. Examples of major and minor changes

Major change	Minor change
Change in business logic affecting output for requests formatted the same way	Added a new endpoint
Removed endpoint	Added a new request parameter
Discontinued support for a request parameter	Added a new response field
Product deprecated	

In addition to deciding what types of changes should be rolled into each version bump, you need to determine how to build API versions into your documentation and how to communicate versions at each level of documentation. Figure 7-5 depicts a banner from Uber's API docs (*https://developer.uber.com/docs/riders/guides/versioning*) that serves this purpose.

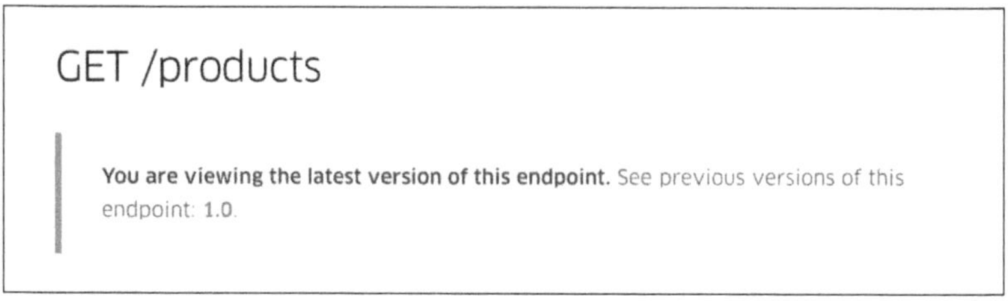

```
GET /products
```

You are viewing the latest version of this endpoint. See previous versions of this endpoint: 1.0.

Figure 7-5. Banner from Uber's API documentation that notifies users about documentation for previous versions of an endpoint

Finally, you might want to incentivize users to adopt new versions by releasing anticipated features with version bumps.

Versioning case study: Stripe

Now that you've explored some of the decisions that you need to make when versioning your API, let's take a look at how Stripe implements versioning. Stripe is an online payments company. Because Stripe as a company relies on third-party developers implementing its API to generate revenue, it is a notable example of a company invested in maintaining backward compatibility. As of 2017, the Stripe API continued to maintain compatibility with every version of its API released since its inception in 2011.

Expert Advice

Shipping frequent improvements to an API is great; breaking something a developer has built is not. Finding an elegant balance is critical—and one way to do it is to entirely avoid breaking changes.

This has been Stripe's approach: we provide backward compatibility to ensure that code written today will still work years from now. We lock the API version that a developer is using once they get started. Unless they actively choose to upgrade (because they want to take advantage of new functionality), we won't require them to do so. Behind the scenes, we introduce discrete programming gates for every new API version. These gates conditionally provide access to new features or changes, isolate layers of logic for requests and responses, and essentially hide any concept of backward compatibility from our main code base.

—Romain Huet, head of developer relations at Stripe

Stripe implements rolling versions, named by the release date. The first time a developer makes an API request, their account is pinned to the most recent API version available. After that, there's no need for requests to specify that pinned version. To upgrade versions, Stripe provides a dashboard where developers have a self-service option to change their default version. Additionally, Stripe allows developers to override the version in individual requests by setting a `Stripe-Version` header, such as `Stripe-Version: 2018-02-28`. This combination of overrides and pinned upgrades allows developers to opt in to changes seamlessly. Interestingly, Stripe has built a */v1* into its API base URIs, even though it has yet to make a major version release with breaking changes. The company has created the opportunity for such a release (*https://stripe.com/blog/api-*

versioning), but as of this writing, it has not yet had to implement one.

Behind the scenes, the Stripe API has codified every possible response with a class called an *API resource*. It has its own domain-specific language, similar to that which defines the possible fields for the resource. When a version change is made, the change is encapsulated in a version change module, which defines documentation about the change, a transformation, and the set of API resource types that are eligible to be modified. The benefit here is that Stripe is able to generate a changelog programmatically as soon as services are deployed with a new version.

Versioning case study: Google+ Hangouts

Next, let's take a look at the Google+ Hangouts API (*https://develop ers.google.com/+/hangouts/release-notes/hangouts-1.2*). In this API, incremental versions were used to communicate groups of changes, not for developers to manage the desired logic or responses of endpoints. Instead, when endpoints needed to be renamed or changed, Google would add a release note indicating that the old endpoint was deprecated (Figure 7-6).

Renamed functions

- ~~getLocale~~ - **Deprecated.** Use getLocalParticipantLocale instead.

- ~~getParticipantId~~ - **Deprecated.** Use getLocalParticipantId instead.

Figure 7-6. Google+ Hangouts API release notes indicating that a function was renamed

Google announced on January 10, 2017, that it would no longer be supporting the API. Apps would run only until April 25, 2017, with a handful of exceptions (Slack, Dialpad, RingCentral, Toolbox, Control Room, and Cameraman). Not only did the company add banners about the announcement throughout its documentation, but it also added a note in the responses stating that the endpoints would no longer work after April 25. Figure 7-7 shows a screenshot of the deprecation banner in the Google+ Hangouts API documentation.

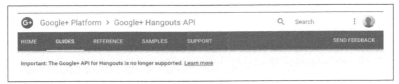

Figure 7-7. Banner for the Google+ Hangouts API indicating that support would be terminated

Process management

Whichever mechanism you choose, versioning adds process overhead to your API. You need to make sure that you have robust documentation to adequately describe the changelog and differences between APIs. Under the hood, you might need to figure out how to deploy versioned code or how to arrange your access control layer to preserve the functionality of older versions. It becomes a nontrivial process to maintain more than one deprecated version, especially if upstream core libraries can affect your API output.

You also want to think about how many versions your staff can support simultaneously. For code maintenance, how will you prioritize security fixes that need to be applied to multiple versions? Will you upgrade all previous versions for certain changes? How will your developer support staff be able to effectively assist developers when they experience issues? These are all considerations that become more complicated and time-consuming with a versioned system.

In some cases, the cost of maintaining versions outweighs the benefits. One of the benefits of not versioning is that you avoid cascading dependencies and complicated maintenance. With only a single layer to your API, the code is transparent and easily readable to your internal developers, and the benefit of maintainability should not be undervalued. You might want to consider delaying versioning until you have adequate infrastructure to support your developers.

Whether you decide to version or not, managing change means finding a balance between maintaining backward compatibility and releasing changes with enough velocity for your developers to succeed on your platform. Don't forget to get feedback, optimize for your developers, and make all changes in moderation.

Closing Thoughts

In this chapter, we discussed many aspects of the continuous process of developing and refining APIs by managing change. Having a strong process and system for managing ongoing changes will be the key to unlocking the full potential of your API. With the ability to manage change, you won't be stuck in the past, and you'll be able to continue improving your API for the future.

In Chapter 8, we tell you all about building a developer ecosystem so that when the time comes to take your API to the next level, you'll have lots of developers waiting to get those new additions.

Building a Developer Ecosystem Strategy

Building a scalable, well-designed API is a great start, but if you want developers to use the API, you need to do much more than just release it. "If you build it, they will come" is a common misconception, as evidenced by the many companies that release APIs but do not understand why developers are not rushing to use them.

The profession of building a developer and partner ecosystem is called *developer relations*. Let's define what an ecosystem is in the context of a developer platform or an API.

Very much like an ecosystem in nature, a developer ecosystem is a virtual system of members that are collaborating, depending, and sometimes competing on the same platform, technology, or API.

There are many examples of developer ecosystems, and some of the best ones are self-organizing—Google and Android have an amazing developer ecosystem and community; iOS developers flock to meetups and collaborate together; and Microsoft has a strong, multifaceted developer and partner ecosystem.

Expert Advice

Developer platforms and APIs have become ubiquitous. They enable developers to be more efficient, leverage existing infrastructure, and future-proof their products and services. As the API economy continues to mature, providing an API is no longer

> enough: companies must offer a truly great developer experience
> and keep pace with developers' needs.
>
> —Romain Huet, head of developer relations at Stripe

In this chapter, we discuss what composes a great ecosystem and how companies building these ecosystems around their APIs do so successfully.

Developers, Developers, Developers

Developers can do great things with an API. They can extend and improve your company's product (Slack apps make Slack better); they can use it and be your clients (Google Cloud Platform is a great example); and they can help with the adoption of your platform/OS (iOS became popular due to the millions of apps on it).

Many companies come to the conclusion that they need an ecosystem after realizing that they cannot build everything themselves. Microsoft cannot build all of the extensions for SharePoint; Google and Apple can't build all the mobile apps themselves; and Slack cannot build all the bots and integrations to its product. These companies open their APIs to developers in order to extend the value of their products.

Other companies use the API as a main way to generate revenue. Companies like Stripe and Cloudinary have the API as the core pillar of their business; they either sell the use of it or charge a fee for certain transactions. In this case, it is really easy to articulate the value of the developer ecosystem.

In this book, *developers* is a general term for people with the technical chops to use your API. They might not identify themselves as developers—they might call themselves an IT person, designer, tech-savvy businessperson, or any variation of engineer. We'll take a look at a few common examples of developers in the subsections that follow.

The Hobbyist

This type of API user is an early adopter who does not necessarily want to use your API professionally. They find joy in playing with the API, creating examples, and trying to find the edge cases and limitations, and they are usually quick to vocalize their opinions.

Hobbyists are usually eager to adopt new features of your API and to give you feedback on its usefulness and quality. The challenge with hobbyists is that sometimes their use cases are not what you are building your API for. If you build an API for facial recognition, the hobbyist will try to use it on cats and dogs. Although this is delightful, it is not your main use case, and you might end up wasting time and resources trying to support low-impact edge uses of your API.

The Hacker

Also called the *early-adopter professional developer* or *entrepreneur*, this is a developer who is trying to put your API to professional use and to potentially make money out of it. The hacker is different from the professional developer who is interested in solving a specific use case and evaluates the API based on product fit adn maturity. In many cases, hackers are the most important audience for your API at its early stage—professional developers, like hobbyists, are eager for new features and willing to deal with changes, but they are also highly focused on solving a concrete use case that is usually aligned with what you thought your API would be used for.

Hackers are **motivated** by innovation; they follow Twitter and scout Medium and Product Hunt to look for new technologies. They might play with a technology because it's cool, but they will always put it to practical use. They are also highly proficient—they can usually deal with a high learning curve and do not need the comfort of SDKs, debugging, or WYSIWYG tools to make use of your API.

The Business-Focused, Tech-Savvy User

This is an audience that is worth mentioning because of its unique characteristics. This developer is interested in only one thing: solving their use case. They might not even consider themselves a developer. They might be a financial person who wants to use your stock price API for their Excel calculations, an IT person who wants to write a script to automate simple workflows, or a businessperson trying to build a website for their company. This audience is extremely sensitive to breaking changes—although using the API is not their day job, they nevertheless need tools and services that will make using your APIs easier, and they will not be following your API news feed on a daily basis.

This audience is important to many companies because it is much larger than the developer audience; there are a lot more business people than developers. If you are targeting this audience, you need to take a very different approach for education and enablement.

The Professional Developer

This type of developer is interested in solving their use case and sees your technology as a means to that end. The professional developer will evaluate your API based on product fit and maturity. They will compare your API to others to see which one meets their needs better. In many use cases this will be the core audience of your API as it matures.

Professional developers are more willing to pay for an API because it solves a problem that would otherwise be a pain to solve. They are eager to see new features but are not keen on changes to the API, especially if these are breaking changes. Professional developers are more sensitive to stability because they recognize the cost associated with getting back and rewriting their code to accommodate your changes. These developers might also have limitations to the time that they can spend building on your API, so they really appreciate tools and services that make doing so easier and faster.

And Many More

There are numerous variations of these audiences—the enterprise developer trying to build internal solutions for their organization, the independent software vendor trying to build software using your API, the contractor whose job is to implement a specification, and many more. They all have different proficiency levels, needs, and wants. As your API matures, you will need to dive in and understand your developer audience and its various segments in more depth.

These are just a few examples of the types of developers you might be targeting as the audience for your API. Some APIs target hardware developers; others are geared for domain-specific developers, such as mobile game developers. It is important to know your audience, the use cases they want to implement using your API, and their preferred means of communication. We cover this type of segmentation work in greater depth later on in this chapter.

Next, let's explore how to build a developer relations strategy. We outline the high-level steps and offer tips and tricks for specific outreach tactics.

Building a Developer Strategy

There are a few basic stages in building a productive developer strategy, beginning with segmenting your developers, determining who your audience is, and defining its attributes. It's also important to distill the value proposition and articulate why developers should use your API/platform. Additionally, you need to outline your developer funnel and itemize the steps that developers should take to be successful with your API.

Next steps include mapping the current and future state of the ecosystem, from where it stands right now to where you'd like to take it. Then you should outline your tactics, such as steps, resources, and actions to move developers through the funnel. Be sure to gather measurements so you can verify that your tactics are working.

Let's dive into each one of these important stages and get the details.

Developer Segmentation

It's time to move on from the anecdotal examples of the different types of developers to a more concrete definition. Ask yourself: who is your audience? In the following subsections, we look at the key attributes you might want to consider.

Identity

How do these developers identify themselves? Frontend? Backend? Full stack? Mobile? Enterprise?

Granular identity can also be very important. In some cases, iOS developers will often connect with other iOS developers at meetups and events, but not as often with Android developers. Some developers, like the members of Google's GDGs, develop a strong sense of identity, whereas others might not be so strongly affiliated.

Developer proficiency

How proficient should a developer be to use your API? Some APIs, such as those for augmented reality and artificial intelligence, might require a steeper learning curve. Sometimes the API is rather simple but requires a complex OAuth and security setup.

Some APIs target developers who are highly proficient, like game developers, whereas others, such as the Google Apps Script API, target a broader audience.

Platform of choice

Mobile developers are very different from web developers, and Xbox and PlayStation game developers are very different from cloud back-end developers. Even within the mobile sphere, iOS developers are quite different from Android developers in the way they build their apps. It is important to understand the platform your developers are on, what the constraints and capabilities of that platform are, and what needs these developers have in common.

Developers tend to identify themselves around platforms—it is very common for Android developers to go to Android Developer Meetups where they encounter like-minded peers. Understanding this will help you engage with your developers where they are—go and give a presentation at their meetup, for example.

Preferred development language, framework, and development tools

Which tools and services does your developer audience use every day to achieve key tasks? If you know their preferred set of programming languages, you may also discover which SDKs you should invest in, for example. The fact that your developers are using Eclipse might be worth knowing when considering building a plug-in to that integrated development environment (IDE). If your developers are avid users of an open source framework, this might lead you to the strategy of becoming a contributor for that framework.

Common use cases and tasks

Even if you are building a very general-purpose API, it is important to know the common use cases are that your developers are trying to accomplish. This can help with building the messaging to these developers and can give you good ideas about how to extend your

API or how to build additional tools or services that can help your developers to achieve their goals. If you do not know which tasks or workloads your developers are trying to accomplish, go out and ask them! You might also use this time to explore key challenges in building these use cases.

Preferred means of communication

This is a critical piece of information if you want to reach your developers. Do they follow your API news on Twitter? Do they prefer email notification? Do they hear about new technologies at events? Do they read an industry news outlet? You need to map ways to communicate day-to-day news and updates and to establish communication channels in case you need to urgently reach your developers.

Market size and geographical distribution

You need to determine how many developers you have right now, and what is the addressable market. You also need to map important centers of developers around the world. This information contributes to the understanding of whether you need to localize your content or run global events, and where to do so.

This is a tricky exercise. It might be difficult or expensive to acquire this information. In many cases a semi-educated guess will work in the beginning, with a more informative analysis conducted as time passes.

Real-life example

Now that we have described the different aspects of audience segmentation, let's examine a concrete example of segmentation analysis.

Table 8-1 shows how the developer segmentation looks for Slack.

Table 8-1. Developer audience segmentation

Attribute	Description
Identity	Enterprise developer (aka IT developer, corporate engineer, internal developer).
Developer proficiency	Proficient at implementing business processes, but not necessarily on the Slack platform. Enterprise developers are used to SDKs and frameworks rather than using the raw APIs.

Attribute	Description
Platform of choice	Windows and Linux scripting, web developers, SharePoint or Confluence.
Preferred development language and frameworks	Java, .NET. Many work with Amazon Web Services (AWS; e.g., AWS Step Functions), some integrate with Slack for reporting. Some developers are exploring Node.js.
Common use cases	Internal use cases—approval processes (time off, expenses, general), reports, and looking up clients in the customer relationship management (CRM) and ticketing systems seem like the most requested set of use cases. Key challenges are that enterprise developers are under a lot of pressure from the business to implement a lot of processes. The current solutions, such as SharePoint, are cumbersome and not developer-friendly, according to them.
Preferred means of communication	Enterprise developers prefer to be notified by email about important changes in our API. They follow Slack's API blog but not the Twitter feed. Major events they are attending are by enterprise software vendors, such as Amazon and IBM.
Market size and geographical distribution	As of May 2018, Slack has more than 200,000 weekly active developers building on the platform (including internal integrations). Major geographical distribution: San Francisco, New York, Tokyo, Berlin, London, Seattle, Bangalore.

Slack actually has two types of developers: app developers (building Slack apps that other teams can use) and enterprise developers (building internal integrations for their own Slack teams).

As with the Slack example, you need to segment each of your audience groups because they might be very different and require different strategies.

This analysis can be much more detailed (and in reality, it usually is) but we hope this demonstrates the different aspects to analyze and the types of answers you are looking for.

Pro Tip

Many startups think that "everyone" is a good segment. It's not! Even the most widely used APIs segment their users; defining your developer audience as "all developers" is not productive.

Distilling the Value Proposition

This could either be very easy or quite difficult, depending on the business you are in. You need to write down the key value proposition of your API. Why should developers use your API, and for what purpose? What is your competitive advantage, and why should developers care about it?

In some cases, platforms put emphasis on different advantages. Google highlights the vast distribution Android has and the number of users with which Android developers can engage, whereas Apple emphasizes the strong ability to monetize iOS and that Apple users are more inclined to pay.

Some APIs provide an easier or more cost-effective way to do something. Cloudinary helps developers create thumbnails and resize images on the fly, and the Google Vision API provides easy access to complex image-recognition functionality.

Here are a few examples of value propositions:

Stripe API
> Provides an easier and more standard way to receive online payments

YouTube API
> Allows you to embed video players in your site or to offer YouTube search capabilities

SoundCloud API
> Lets you develop apps that allow users to upload and share songs online

Some companies have distinct value propositions for different developer segments, and that's fine. For example, AWS can be a place for rapid prototyping for startups, as well as a way to drive technical transformation in big enterprises.

Your value proposition is closely related to the use case your developers are trying to implement. If you do not know what your major use cases are going to look like, try to find out; it will help you home in on a value proposition.

After you define your value proposition, you can validate whether it is compelling. One company, for example, said that it could run an operation in less than 10 milliseconds, whereas all its competitors took 30 milliseconds. Although this sounds impressive, it requires validation because it might not be important to developers implementing common web use cases—30 milliseconds might be sufficient, and the performance improvement might not merit the migration cost. Alternatively, this might be a key enabling feature for some use cases that might be worth a lot of money.

A value proposition is not the same as marketing "positioning." Whereas market position refers to the consumer's perception of a brand or product, value proposition should be concrete and, preferably, something the developers care deeply about. The words you pick are not that important at this stage; the actual value is.

A common mistake that many companies initially make is creating a lot of low-value statements—the product is "a little cheaper in some cases" or "a little easier to use on X." Although these are useful benefits, you should strive for a big and compelling value for your developers, when possible.

Expert Advice

There should be a significant amount of value offered to those building on your API. That value doesn't have to be directly monetizable, but the API has to do something better, faster, or more cheaply than if the third-party developer or partner were to build the same thing in house.

—Chris Messina, developer experience lead at Uber

Defining Your Developer Funnel

The *developer funnel* is a simple but effective concept that outlines the journey that a developer goes through, from not knowing about your API to becoming an avid and successful user.

Figure 8-1 depicts an example of a developer funnel.

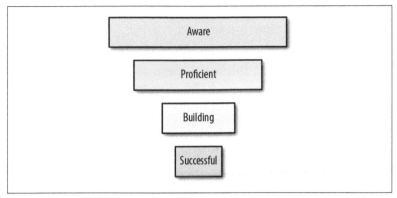

Figure 8-1. The developer funnel

As you can see in Figure 8-1, in each step of the funnel, there are fewer and fewer developers. Your job is to get more developers into the funnel and to then move them down through it. Let's explore the different stages:

Aware

Creating developer awareness is an ongoing and important first step in the developer funnel. After you build your API, making developers aware of it and its unique and compelling value proposition is the beginning of the developer funnel. Many organizations with mature and successful APIs still work to ensure their visibility to the developer community. The creators of Twilio, a popular API providing a cloud communications platform for building SMS, voice, and messaging applications, still pay for advertisements across Silicon Valley.

Proficient

Next, developers need to know how to use the API. They could reference your guide on how to build a simple "Hello World" app or take a comprehensive training and certification program. (We explore these in Chapter 9.) The end game in this step is that the developer can easily use your API according to your documented best practices.

Building

At this stage, the developer is actively building apps using your API. For example, the code might not yet be in production, but the API keys are actively used. This is an important step in the funnel because it signals that the value proposition that you have outlined is the right one.

Successful

For each developer, this could mean something different. The definition of success could also vary for each API usage. The successful usage of your API could mean making money out of it or passing a certain threshold of usage. Or it might be defined as passing transactions in production or even the API's integration with other systems. You need to determine what success means for your API and your developer audience. We talk about measurements in "Deriving Measurements" on page 160.

Funnel indicators

Not all developer funnels have the same milestones. Some funnels might have a "Developer Registered" stage, while others might have "Developer Signed the Terms" or "Developer Paid for the API" as significant events that separately mark the various phases of the funnel. You need to build your own developer funnel and define its steps for your specific API.

No matter which milestone steps you choose in your funnel, it is important that you outline the funnel and understand the key indicators that reflect these steps. Table 8-2 presents some example indicators.

Table 8-2. Funnel indicators

Aspect	Indicator examples
Awareness	Getting into your API website, registering for a newsletter, attending a meetup
Proficiency	Completing a hands-on lab, building a fun hackathon project, creating an open source example, executing a "Hello World" sample
Usage	Creating an API key and using it, deploying a sample app and modifying it, creating and running a preproduction environment
Success	Generating revenue, moving code to production, getting users, building a business, actively using the API 150 times per day

We use these examples to build the strategy measurements later in this chapter, but you can already see that these indicators are moving the needle in your developer strategy dashboard.

Mapping the Current and Future State

Now that you have a good understanding of the developer funnel and the indicators that tie to it, you need to know the *current actual numbers* for each indicator.

Table 8-3 offers an example of a report that you might be able to generate for an API that adds a filter to images as a service.

Table 8-3. Key indicators status report

Aspect	Monthly ongoing status	Totals
Awareness	500 unique users a month on *api.imagefilters.com*	10,000 unique developers to date
Proficiency	200 developers have gone through the getting started stage	5,000 unique developers to date
Usage	50 developers have moved to the *Pro* edition	1,500 paying developers to date
Success	500,000 images processed by new developers	250 million images processed to date

As you can see, some of the measurements might be directly connected to a number of developers, whereas others might be derived from developer usage. In this example, the number of images processed is derived from the success of the developers using the API.

Sometimes, the funnel indicator is derived rather than direct—you can see in Table 8-3 that you might be able to affect the last number (250 million images processed to date) without getting new developers. You might be able to work with current developers to get them to use your API more. That is true with a lot of APIs, and some of the tactics that we outline in the next section should target current developers, not necessarily new ones.

Next, we need to add two additional columns:

Market potential
    What are the long-term goals for each indicator?

Short-term targets
    What are we trying to achieve in the short term?

Mapping the market potential is somewhat of a guess. It is sometimes really difficult to determine what the addressable market is. You can buy market research, go to developer communities that might be potential users and assess their size, or ask colleagues who have similar addressable markets. Big companies like Google, Amazon, and Facebook release developer size and usage metrics that might be good benchmarks for you if you are addressing the same developers. You can also use the sizing determinations you made when segmenting your developer audiences. See "Market size and geographical distribution" on page 149.

Now that you know what the market potential is, you can set short-term targets. These targets will influence the tactics you use in the next section of this chapter.

Let's add the short-term targets and market potential columns to Table 8-3. Table 8-4 presents the results.

Table 8-4. Key indicators with short-term targets and market potential

Aspect	Monthly ongoing status	Q2 targets	Market potential
Awareness	500 unique users a month on *api.imagefilters.com*	Grow to 700	500,000 developers
Proficiency	200 developers have gone through the getting started stage	Grow to 400	250,000 developers
Usage	50 developers have moved to the *Pro* edition	Grow to 70	150,000 developers
Success	500,000 images processed by new developers	Grow to 700,000	50,000 developers

Outlining Your Tactics

Now that you know what the current status is and where you want to be in the short and long term, it is time to map the tactical steps you are planning to take to move developers through the funnel. Here are a set of examples of tactics to use in each step in the funnel that we previously outlined.

Awareness tactics examples

Awareness tactics need to move developers from not knowing about an API to knowing about it and hopefully being excited about using it. Here are some examples of activities that can drive awareness:

- Build an API documentation site.
- Run a Facebook ad campaign to drive developers to the site.

- Create swag that developers love, adorned with the logo of your API/platform.
- Have a booth at a big developer event.
- Contribute to a popular open source project with content relevant to your API.
- Write an article in an industry news outlet.
- Run a Product Hunt campaign.
- Speak at events.

Proficiency tactics examples

Proficiency tactics aim to educate developers about how to use the API, from the basics to the best practices. Here are some examples of activities that can drive proficiency:

- Write tutorials about getting started and different aspects of your API.
- Create hands-on code labs.
- Build code samples, templates, and SDKs.
- Run hackathons.
- Build a certification program for developers.
- Write whitepapers.
- Run webinars.

Usage tactics examples

Usage tactics drive developers to use the API in production, expanding the current use cases and promoting new types of API use. Here are some examples of activities that can drive usage:

- Build a registration system with which developers can manage their API usage.
- Build a coupon or free-tier system to incentivize production usage.
- Run a design sprint with a partner to build product-level API usage.
- Run a beta program for new API features.

- Run a feedback program to capture ways to improve usage.

Success tactics examples

Success tactics drive the developer's own goals, whether those are making money, improving their business, or technical goals such as high availability. One useful strategy is to let successful developers teach other developers how your API helped them to reach their own goals. Here are some examples of activities that can drive developer success:

- Run a comarketing campaign with selected developers.
- Write content with successful developers to share tips and tricks for using your API.
- Add a best practices section to your developer site.
- Run API optimization workshops.
- Create a top developer program that identifies successful developers and highlights their achievements.

These are just a few examples of developer relations tactics; in Chapter 9, we discuss building and running such developer programs at greater length. You might have a totally different set of steps to get your ecosystem going and flourishing. The important part is that you are strategic and thoughtful in outlining your tactics.

 Pro Tip

It is easy to confuse tactics and the steps associated with them. Some people might think that they can achieve developer success through hackathons, while hackathons actually contribute to developer proficiency, for example. This leads to frustration and loss of productivity. Make sure you do the proper actions to move the right metrics.

You probably don't want to immediately execute all the tactics we just outlined. Some things, like providing documentation and a way to register for API keys, are usually table stakes, but a lot of these activities are optional. Next, you need to pick and choose the right set of activities to help you achieve your short-term goals.

Here is an example of a developer relations high-level quarterly plan that maps targets to tactics:

- Increase developer awareness to 5,000 new developers.
  - *Tactic:* Run a developer marketing campaign.
  - *Tactic:* Release two articles in major news outlet(s).
- Increase developer proficiency to 1,000 new developers.
  - *Tactic:* Run two workshops in developer events, with 300 developers in each.
  - *Tactic:* Build a new front page to the developer site, with a better call to action to get started.
  - *Tactic:* Create five tutorials that outline common use cases.
- Drive 40 new developers to use their API keys in production.
  - *Tactic:* Work with sales to identify 20 candidates and run design sprints with these developers.
  - *Tactic:* Run a beta program for our new Thumbnail feature with 20 launch partners.
- Grow the number of image process API calls to 150,000.
  - *Tactic:* Work with the top five developers to increase their API usage.
  - *Tactic:* Write an article with two developers that are successfully using our API.

Many companies go through prioritization exercises and pick the top goals and activities every quarter. Many organizations, including Google, highly recommend and find it effective to structure these plans in a format called objective key results (OKRs) (*https://rework.withgoogle.com/guides/set-goals-with-okrs/steps/introduction/*).

When you first build your API, the plan should be very straightforward. You need to ask yourself, "What are the things developers *must* have before using our API?" These will probably include documentation, basic samples, and a developer landing page. As time passes and you get these initial table-stakes tasks done, you can start asking yourself, "What are the things developers *should* have in order to be proficient and successful at using our API?"

Deriving Measurements

You have a plan and you can now begin executing it, right? Well… yes, but we recommend one additional step before you get started. One of the most difficult challenges is connecting developer activities to measurements. We talked about the current state and future state, but how do you know that you are going in the right direction and that what you are doing is impactful?

The key here is to think hard about what the metric is that you want to affect when running each activity and then to measure whether you actually hit your targets at the end of each activity. For example, when hosting an event, you can measure the number of developers who actually run a hands-on lab and follow up on that cohort to see if they turn into active developers. After a *design sprint* (a structured activity in which the team brainstorms and prototypes solutions), you can measure whether the partner has actually implemented the sprint's recommendation, thus improving or extending their API usage. Some activities are more difficult to track, but it is critical to try to measure each of the activities and to evaluate whether they've moved the needle.

Table 8-5 lists a few examples of key performance indicators (KPIs) and how you can connect them to activities.

Table 8-5. Developer activities measurement report

Measurement	KPI	Current	Goal	Activity	Expected impact	Actual
Developer awareness	Website entry	10,000	100,000	Speak at SXSW	5,000 new developers	7,000
Proficiency	Token created	5,000	10,000	Run a technical webcast	5,000 new tokens	3,000

You can be creative with your activities and explore many ways to affect your KPIs, but we recommend keeping them consistent so that you can track your impact over time.

Pro Tip

Building a thriving ecosystem is like gardening. You cannot be sure which activity will be successful with a particular set of circumstances. By measuring, iterating, and improving, you can learn what is impactful and what is not.

Closing Thoughts

Building a developer strategy is all about knowing what to measure and which actions affect your measurements and goals. Following the process that we have outlined in this chapter will help you to clearly define your developer strategy, and all the rest will be building and executing it.

Expert Advice

You need to know your users, their needs and use cases, and tune the API accordingly.

It's important to keep the communication channels with your users open and transparent. This is critical to get feedback and improve the API. You need to nurture your ecosystem and put in a lot of effort in order to make it grow and be successful.

—Ido Green, developer advocate at Google

In Chapter 9, we discuss how to build and execute developer relations programs. We cover community programs and documentation, and we learn from the experience of companies such as Facebook, Google, and others about what works and what doesn't.

CHAPTER 9

Developer Resources

Building a great API is not enough if no one knows how to use it. As you design your API, make sure that you guide and enable developers by providing the learning materials they need to succeed.

Developer resources are a set of assets that you should provide your developers so that they can improve how they use your API. There are many types of developer resources out there, each affecting different aspects of the development life cycle. In this chapter, we cover the major resources that most companies provide. We also provide some tips and tricks to make them work for you.

API Documentation

Let's begin with the most basic resource that is required for every API or platform—documentation.

Documentation is where developers come to learn about your API. Whether you're providing a simple *README* file or developing a full website for your developers, it is critical to clearly document how they can most effectively use your API. There are several different aspects to good documentation, covering all stages of the development life cycle.

Getting Started

Getting Started guides are a common type of tutorial that walk the developer from unfamiliarity with an API to initial success. In many cases, this comes in the form of completing a "Hello World" exercise

—a reference to the common practice within the engineering profession of getting a program or API to churn out "Hello World" as a proof of success. The API doesn't literally have to return "Hello, world", but you might have users get to a place where they've successfully made one API request, opened a WebSocket connection and received the first event, or received an example POST request from a WebHook. The Getting Started tutorial's job is to outline the easiest and fastest set of steps that developers need to take to get there, also known as the *Time to Hello World* (TTHW).

Having a Getting Started guide that you position front and center on your API site is important for onboarding new developers. Simplifying and shortening the TTHW significantly contributes to developer adoption of your API.

A single Getting Started guide works for simple use cases, but if you have a complex API that covers multiple use cases, you should augment your initial guide with additional primers that expand on it. You could have several Getting Started tutorials, each focusing on different aspect—for example, "Building Your First Web App," "Getting Started Storing Your Data," and "Introducing User Authentication."

Here are some key aspects of a good Getting Started guide:

Do not assume prior knowledge
As much as you can, try to explain each technical term in your document. (You can do that using links to other pages or pop-up windows, to refer the user to more in-depth literature on specific topics.) If there are prerequisites, provide links to their corresponding Getting Started documents.

Do not diverge from the happy path
Assume that everything will go well, but link to troubleshooting documentation for cases in which something goes wrong. Don't leave developers high and dry, without the answers and off the happy path.

Show examples of inputs and outputs
If the developer needs to run a command line, show an example of that command line; if there is an expected result, show a screenshot of that result.

Your API might have several function calls, different types of requests (POST/GET), and different responses and parameters.

Show every permutation of each method and the corresponding outputs.

Try to show sample code demonstrating the simplest use of your API
If it is not too long or cumbersome, provide samples that demonstrate basic use of the code.

End with a call to action and links to other references
Don't let your developers become stuck; be sure to give them a direction and resources to help them expand their knowledge.

Expert Advice

The right API design creates engaging and delightful developer experiences, and a well-thought-out onboarding process is critical for developers to instantly understand how the API operates and rapidly build on it. For example, Stripe's dynamic and personalized developer documentation provides customized code samples that can be quickly added to an existing application, and we offer first-class libraries in popular programming languages. API endpoints, parameters, data models, and error messages are all carefully defined and consistent across the platform. Developer support is also part of the core product experience, and we work hard to provide a response within hours (or minutes). We believe that these touch points produce an elegant API design that ensures developers are successful, exponentially improving their productivity.

If you look back 10 years, starting a business and accepting payments online was incredibly hard. There was no other choice than to build in-house solutions, establish merchant accounts, and read through hundreds of pages of documentation just to accept a simple payment. At Stripe, we see payments as a problem rooted in code, not finance. Our API design allows developers to accept payments from anywhere in the world, using any payment methods, in a matter of minutes.

—Romain Huet, head of developer relations at Stripe

API Reference Documentation

This is a very technical part of the documentation and might be automated using tools like Swagger. Reference documents like the one shown in Figure 9-1 are detailed descriptions of all the API methods, their input and output parameters, and the errors that they might return.

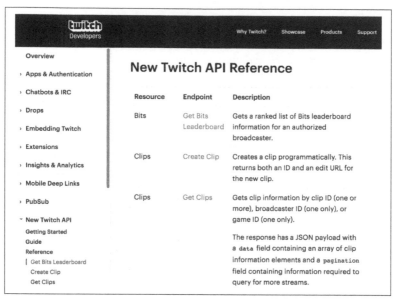

Figure 9-1. Twitch's API reference page

Reference documentation should be comprehensive and complete. Do not worry about repeating common sections, because these types of documents are not intended to be read in sequence. For example, if you have an error that appears in two methods, it is important to repeat the error description and causes in both sections because developers are not necessarily going to read through documentation for every API endpoint. Reference documents are also a great place to put examples of the API usage and even to add a built-in API tester so that developers can begin experimenting with the API. We go over API testers in more depth in "Sandboxes and API Testers" on page 179.

Because users will usually access these pages from Google search or from your own internal search, it is better to list each API method on its own page. This improves discoverability and usability. Additionally, it gives you greater flexibility to provide more detail when necessary.

Good reference documents provide developers with everything they need to know about a certain API call or functionality within a single page, with links to useful additional resources.

Tutorials

In this section of your documentation, you provide step-by-step instructions for different aspects of your API, as illustrated in Figure 9-2. You can write an article about security or rate limits, for example. Begin by covering the complex parts of your API and then move to more simple things, if you have the bandwidth.

API tutorials

These tutorials aim to help you get the most from your experience developing on Shopify's API.

- **Building an application** – If you've never built an app before, this tutorial will walk you through code examples of what is required to authenticate and make basic API calls.

- **Building a Node.js application** – Use Node.js and Express to build an app that connects to a Shopify store, requests a permanent access token, and makes an API call to the authenticated shop endpoint using that access token.

- **Adding billing to your app** – Use Shopify's Billing API to charge users for your app.

Figure 9-2. Shopify's API tutorials

Pro Tip

A good best practice here is to work with your support team and ask them which topics generate the greatest number of tickets. You can use that information to create tutorials on the topics that are the most difficult for your audience. Doing this periodically will ensure that you are always documenting high-frequency issuess.

It is important to remember that you need to update tutorials when you update your API, or you risk them becoming misleading rather than a source of guidance for developers. You can also sort them based on metainformation, such as the programming language used in the tutorial. This makes it easier for your developers to find what they need.

Frequently Asked Questions

In a similar vein, collect frequently asked questions (FAQ) and answer them to the best of your ability. Remember to generalize and anonymize the questions and answers. The format of the FAQ document is simple: put the question in the bold and the answer below it, as demonstrated in Figure 9-3. If you like, you can prefix these with "Q:" and "A:," respectively.

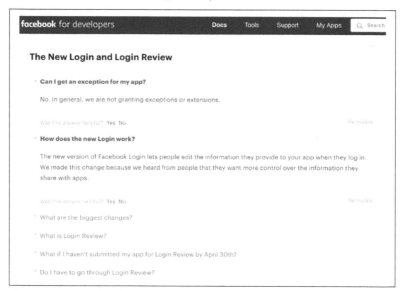

Figure 9-3. Facebook API FAQ page

There are many ways to collect a list of frequently asked questions. Here are a few examples:

- Have a monthly meeting with the support team and ask what the most common tickets are.

- Explore Stack Overflow and look for the most voted for question around your API.

- Talk to the partnership and sales team and ask what questions they hear the most.

- Ask developers to add to your FAQ section by inviting them to submit questions in a form that you should make available on that page.

Landing Page

This is the first page developers should see when they view your documentation site. It should generally have the following sections:

- A short explanation of what your API is for (see "Distilling the Value Proposition" on page 151). Walk through the use cases the developer can implement or the key value they can get from the API.

- A call to action that directs the developer to next steps. "Get Started" is a great call to action, with a link to the Getting Started document.

- Links to key resources, samples, and tools, all of which we describe later on in this chapter.

Your developer landing page serves two purposes: it welcomes and onboards new developers, and it provides resources and ongoing support to returning developers. You might want to collaborate with your marketing or design team to make sure that the page is appealing and designed for both audiences.

This page is extremely important because it provides the first impression of the API. Developers will skim through this page to see whether it is the right fit for their needs and will quickly bounce out if they do not find what they want. Slack has gone through several iterations, each time improving a different aspect of the landing page. Google has spent week at a time doing user research to optimize its developer portal. Stripe has done a good job with its documentation landing page, as you can see in Figure 9-4.

Figure 9-4. Stripe's API landing page

Pro Tip

Make sure your landing page and other key pages are highly discoverable in search engines such as Google. This will be the most common way developers find your site.

Changelog

As your API evolves and matures, we recommend that you keep a changelog on your developer site. On this page, you provide developers with news about updates to the API, details on breaking changes that might be coming, security and service change notifications, and so forth.

Pro Tip

GitHub Releases (*https://help.github.com/articles/creating-releases/*) make it easy to create changelogs. Check out the Releases API for more details.

Adding an RSS feed to the page enables developers to subscribe to the changelog and to be notified when you update it, as depicted in Figure 9-5. This is a simple way to create a channel for developers to keep up to date with your API.

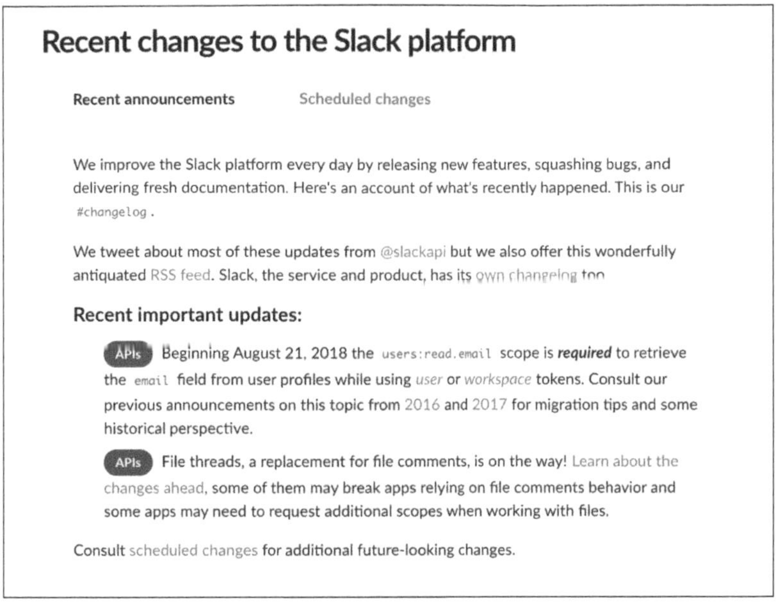

Figure 9-5. Slack API changelog

Changes to your code can also be announced in an email or over Twitter, if you can reach your developers that way. However, a dedicated page that lets developers see all the changes that your API has gone through since they last touched it can also be very useful. Remember that different audiences prefer different means of communication, as discussed in Chapter 8.

Terms of Service

The terms of service (ToS) is a document that describes the reasonable use of your API—what is permitted and, more importantly, what is not permitted. This document is very useful for developers who want to understand whether their use case is supported, but it is also critical for you as the API developer in order to set the boundaries of usage of your API. The ToS is the baseline for enforcement—taking action against misuse of your API. Without knowing what is permitted and what is not, developers may find it difficult to know how to act like good citizens on your platform.

The ToS should be written, or at least reviewed, by your legal counsel. The document should define things like the following:

Rate limits
> See Chapter 6 for more details on rate-limiting.

Data retention policy
> How long and for what can a developer use the data they get from your API?

Privacy policy
> What can developers do with personally identifiable information (PII)? With whom can they share it?

Non-allowed use cases
> Can your API be used for commercial use cases? Can it be used for adult or gambling use cases?

API license
> Can developers resell your API? Can they use it as part of their API? Is it free to use?

Additional requirements
> Should the developers post privacy acknowledgments in their apps?

There may be many more aspects for you to cover in your ToS. It is also important to state in the ToS that you can change the terms as time passes. As your ecosystem grows and your API evolves, you will find that you need to update your ToS to adjust to the new circumstances.

When communicating with developers who have misused your API, you should refer to the section in your ToS that they violated and work with them to reach compliance.

Pro Tip

Remember that to be effective, your ToS should be simple and short. It's a legal document that you actually want developers to read and understand, not a ritualized checkbox.

Samples and Snippets

Providing developers with code samples and snippets is a great way to improve their use of and productivity with your API. When done right, you can incorporate best practices (such as for performance and security), into your examples, making the developers less prone to make errors with or misuse the API.

Code Samples

Code samples can take a wide range of forms, but they all follow the basic intent of providing developers with reference examples of how to use the API. You should provide code samples in the programming languages most common to your developers. The code should be highly readable and include a lot of comments that walk the developer through the code and explain each section of the API's use.

Even if you can only provide a single code sample, that can be valuable to developers of all backgrounds, assuming that it's consistent and based on core development principles. PHP and Node.js are great for these kinds of examples for web APIs because they're easy to focus on request and response cycles without the need to reference any additional frameworks.

Pro Tip

Just like tutorials and documents, code samples need to be maintained. When the API changes, you need to update all of your examples too.

Most code samples try to tackle a single use case of the API, like sending a message, getting an event, or making a payment. Other code samples provide examples of integrations between different aspects of your API, such as illustrating an authenticated request to an API or combining the responses from two requests to accomplish a task, for example.

Another type of code sample is the *reference app*. This code sample tackles a business use case rather than demonstrating specific API functionality. Good examples of these are the open source Google I/O app, which Google releases every year, or the chat app that Twitch built into its sample.

The major challenge with reference apps is making them readable, usable, and not too tightly connected to the use case. If an app is super-optimized for the use case, it is difficult for a developer to learn from it and to extrapolate what they need to implement their own use case.

Snippets

Snippets, on the other hand, are short and contextual code samples that accompany a tutorial, a reference doc, or an FAQ answer. Snippets should be in the single digits of lines of code, and they need to be briefly documented but still very readable.

Unlike code samples, snippets are a part of complete code; you do not need to declare variables or add imports to a snippet. The snippet should look like it has been cut out of a code sample and pasted into the document, as depicted in Figure 9-6.

```
12 function impostaCookie (nome, valore, percorso, scadenza) {
13   valore=escape(valore);
14
15   if (scadenza == "") {
16      var oggi = new Date();
17      oggi.setMonth(oggi.getMonth()+6);
18      scadenza=oggi.toGMTString();
19   }
20   if (percorso!="")
21      percorso= ";Path=" + percorso;
22
23   document.cookie = nome + "=" + valore + ";expires=" + scadenza + percorso;
24 }
25
```

Figure 9-6. A snippet

Because snippets are shorter and easier to implement, we recommend that you implement them in several programming languages to make it easy for developers to cut and paste directly into their own code.

A good method here is to use an interactive language switcher in your documentation that lets the developer choose their preferred programming language, as shown in Figure 9-7.

Figure 9-7. Firebase samples with language switcher

Software Development Kits and Frameworks

Developers have different proficiency levels, and not all of them will be comfortable accessing your web API directly. As discussed in "Developer SDKs" on page 114, building software development kits (SDKs) and frameworks is a good way to make it easier to access your API. Another benefit of a good SDK or framework is that you can bake best practices and security measurements straight into them. Creating these boilerplate code blocks removes the need for developers to implement these best practices themselves.

Expert Advice

A good API has SDK bindings in all languages, platforms, and coding styles. One of the lessons I learned is that you have to be prepared in advance for extreme use cases and make sure that your API can meet the needs of customers.

—Ron Reiter, senior director of engineering at Oracle

SDKs

SDKs are thin abstraction layers over your API. They provide developers with the ability to work with a code library rather than making raw API calls. Developers download or refer to an SDK library and build their business logic by calling the functionality of the SDK.

Many companies wrap their APIs with SDKs, and many developers prefer to use an SDK rather than calling the API methods directly. This is due to the inherent complexity that comes with handling and making web requests.

The interfaces of the SDK need to be readable and well documented, but the internals of the SDK do not need to meet these requirements. The internals of the SDK library can be optimized or even obfuscated and minified.

It is important that you provide SDKs in the programming language(s) your developers use. SDKs are not like sample code; they are less portable and basically useless if they are not in the programming language of your audience.

Remember that, after you launch an SDK, you need to continue to update it. The key here is to update your SDK at the same time you make your API updates. Assuming that your developers are relying heavily on your SDK, if you do not update it, they will not have access to the new platform or API features that you just launched.

Pro Tip

It is important to instrument and measure the use of your SDK separately from measuring direct API calls. Building and maintaining multiple SDKs is expensive and demanding. Looking at the data gives you a good indication of whether you need to continue to invest in your SDKs.

You can generate SDKs automatically by using tools such as Swagger. There is some infrastructure work involved in enabling such tools (such as adding metadata to your API), but this can be an easy and productive way to generate SDKs in multiple programming languages.

Expert Advice

Cloudinary's APIs are the main way our customers use us besides the administration web console. Developers building websites and apps that involve any type of imagery and video use us to upload, manipulate, manage, and deliver the media. The API is RESTful and is wrapped by numerous SDKs, available in almost any programming language.

—Ran Rubinstein, VP of solutions at Cloudinary

For more information on the technical aspects of an SDK, see Chapter 6.

Frameworks

Frameworks are additional layers of abstraction that you sometimes need to add over an API. They make it easier to use API methods by providing functionality that is closer to the use case the developer needs to implement and can further hide the complexity of the API.

A good example is the Botkit framework. When Slack initially released its API, it provided basic functionality to read and write messages. Although this was all the functionality that experienced developers needed to build Slack apps, it did not provide an easy way to build conversational interfaces and bots. Developers had to handle complex use cases, such as asking for user inputs in Slack and waiting for the answers to come back through the API.

The Botkit team developed an open source framework that encapsulated that functionality and wrapped the complexity of these use cases in a simple and easy-to-use library, as illustrated in Example 9-1. Developers using the Botkit framework more easily coded their way through these challenging use cases by letting Botkit handle these processes.

Example 9-1. Botkit framework snippet

```
controller.hears(
    ['hello', 'hi', 'greetings'],
    ['direct_mention', 'mention', 'direct_message'],
    function(bot,message) {
        bot.reply(message.'Hello!');
    }
);
```

As you can see in Example 9-1, the developer states that they are looking to *hear* hello, hi, or greetings by way of a mention, direct mention, or direct message, and what they reply with, in turn, is Hello! This would have been an order of magnitude more complex to code if it weren't for the Botkit framework. With Botkit, the developer just defines the business process, and the framework takes care of all the rest.

Sometimes, you don't need an opinionated framework. If your API is simple and intuitive, you might want to reduce maintenance cost by just providing code samples or SDKs, and leave the additional complexity to your developers. You might also take into account the proficiency of your developers. Advanced developers might not need a framework in order to handle complex use cases.

When maintained correctly, frameworks and SDKs provide an easier path to API upgrades and migrations. You as the API provider can abstract the API changes and let the developers keep their old code working. Breaking changes have a smaller negative impact if the only thing the developer needs to do is to replace the SDK or framework with a new version. The same goes for new functionality: developers can easily access new API calls using the same known paradigm just by replacing the old SDK or framework with a new version that supports the new functionality.

When building SDKs and frameworks, it is important to make them accessible and discoverable on your API site. We also recommend that you host your SDKs and frameworks in code repositories such as GitHub so that developers can be inspired by the code, report bugs, and contribute if needed. See "Community Contribution" on page 182 for more on this topic.

Development Tools

Your API can easily look like a taunting black box to your developers. Providing the right tools can go a long way toward helping developers solve their own problems. It is not easy to generalize the types of tools your API might need. Each API comes with a different set of challenges. There are some common pain points, which we cover here, but you need to analyze and understand your developers' needs and pains and to define tools specifically for your service.

Debugging and Troubleshooting

In Chapter 4, we discussed how to make errors meaningful so that developers can better understand whether a request fails due to something they did wrong or due to an issue with the system. However, even with meaningful errors, it can still be difficult for developers to know exactly how and why their request failed.

That's why providing developers with tools to analyze, debug, and troubleshoot their API calls can therefore be very helpful.

Debugging tools can be as simple as a web page that lets the developer see the logs that are associated with their API calls or as complicated as a step-by-step debugger that integrates into the development environment. In many cases, the former is good enough to troubleshoot most issues.

Sandboxes and API Testers

Sandboxes and API testers give developers the ability to quickly test and verify that they are using the API in the right way. Sandboxes provide developers with a safe and isolated environment—for example, a mocked-up list of images that they can delete and modify as they want, using the API, without the worry of changing product data. API testers usually come as part of the API documentation and let developers test the API calls—sometimes on live data. Google provides a very comprehensive API testing service called APIs Explorer. Figure 9-8 presents an example of an API test page.

Figure 9-8. Google's APIs Explorer

Note that developers do not need to code in order to make an API request using APIs Explorer; they just need to provide valid input parameters.

Rich Media

There are many ways to learn technical content—some people like to read, some like to listen, and some like to watch. Although a lot of developers prefer written tutorials and documents, there is a growing trend of engaging and educating developers via short videos, webinars, live Q&A sessions, and so forth.

Videos

Videos are a great way to introduce new tech, provide general best practices, or deep dive into a topic.

These days, creating videos is not that difficult—most phones and digital cameras can create high-definition videos. Many developer relations people even create video tutorials from the comfort of their own homes.

That said, although creating and editing videos is getting easier, making high-quality videos can still be expensive and difficult: you need professional gear, a lot of practice, and several rehearsals. At Google there is a full team dedicated to editing and producing videos. Presenting in these videos is not something that every developer relations person is fit to do. It requires a certain skill to be in front of a camera and to present content that is complex and involves screens that you don't actually see while standing in front of a green screen.

Pro Tip

The best-performing videos are short. Videos longer than two minutes tend to have a drastic drop in viewership.

If you are happy with medium-quality videos, recording live sessions is a great way to get started. Whenever you do a live presentation at an event, you can record the session and use that on your website for other developers to see.

Storytime: Doubling Down on Video

When I worked at Google, we decided to double down on videos after a very long global tour during which we presented the same content again and again in more than 12 countries. We recorded some of the sessions and found that the recordings reached a greater number of people (measured in number of views) than our total accumulated live audience throughout the tour. After that, we created an entire team dedicated to generating high-quality videos at scale.

—Amir Shevat

Office Hours

Office hours are a great resource for developers to get their questions answered. This is a block of time that you set aside to answer questions and help developers build on your API.

When the Slack Developer Platform team launched, it was very small. Team members could not meet all the developers who wanted them to provide training on the platform in person and decided to launch a weekly office hours online. Developers and partners could join the office hours using a public video call link, provided by Slack, and ask their questions. Because these sessions had multiple participants, they had the added value of having everyone learn from one another's questions.

Webinars and Online Training

Webinars are a good way to educate developers online. In fact, some developers prefer this way of learning because it is somewhat more collaborative. In webinars, the speaker presents a topic through an online tool, such as Zoho, and invites developers to join the training. The presentation is broadcast to the audience, sometimes accompanied by screen sharing or videos. At the end of the webinar, and sometimes even during the webinar, developers can ask questions on the content, and the presenter answers them.

> ### Expert Advice
>
> As of this writing, I run a monthly web training session about my previous book, *Designing Bots* (O'Reilly). The webinar takes two hours, and participants go through training and hands-on exercises. I get to engage with about 50 developers without leaving the comfort of my office.
>
> —Amir Shevat

Community Contribution

Although all of the resources we outlined in this chapter are great ways to educate, train, and engage developers to use your API, building out all these resources is a difficult task that requires time and money. But fear not! Some of these resources can be created and maintained by the community of developers that use your API.

One of the positive side effects of a thriving developer community is that its members contribute content and generate resources. Developers write tutorials, create videos, share code samples, and answer questions. Here are a few real-world examples of these types of contribution:

- Google works with key members of the community called Google Developers Experts to create everything from videos and presentations to code samples.
- Slack manages open source SDKs and receives bug fixes and code patches on an ongoing basis. It also lists community articles on its own developer site.

- Mobile developers meet around the world, share insights, and train one another. In Tel Aviv, Israel, for example, a group of community members who have created a volunteer-run course called Android Academy that educates new developers on how to build great Android apps.
- Twitch uses public forums in which developers can talk about work they have done, support one another, and provide feedback to the Twitch Developer Experience product team.

Almost every API out there has some community contribution. Remember that you will need to provide the basic documentation yourself, because in the beginning, community contribution will be minimal. Consider the community contribution as an addition to your work, not a replacement of it.

Pro Tip

Whenever you are using community-contributed content, give credit to the contributor. They have done a selfless act for you, and giving them props for that is both the right thing to do and an inspiration to others who want to contribute.

Building a section for community contribution in your developer site is a great way to empower your developers, once you have enough articles and code samples there. Remember that maintenance is a bigger issue with community contribution; if you change your API, work with your contributors to amend their content or to clearly state the version for which each contribution is good.

Closing Thoughts

Developer resources add a delicate and crucial layer of value over your API. Without developer resources, your audience needs to guess how to use your API and will probably misuse it—or, more commonly, just not use it at all.

In this chapter, we outlined common developer resources and gave tips on how to build them. Remember that each API is different, and your developers might need an additional set of resources that we haven't explicitly covered here. Keep in touch with your developers, empathize with them, and foster your community to build a self-sustaining ecosystem.

In Chapter 10, we discuss exactly that: how to build developer programs that foster a thriving ecosystem. Let's dive into that now.

Developer Programs

So, you've built the basic resources developers will need to use your API or platform—are you done yet? Probably not. As we discussed in Chapter 8, driving developers through the funnel and helping them to become aware, proficient, engaged, and successful using your API is an ongoing process. Even well-adopted APIs, such as the most commonly used ones provided by Amazon and Google, require ongoing activity by their developer relations teams. Developer programs are the heart and soul of everyday developer relations and ecosystem building for an API.

Defining Your Developer Programs

Developer programs are activities that help and drive developers of all sizes to build solutions and integrate with your API. Most companies offer multiple developer programs through their developer relations and marketing teams. To define the developer programs that you need to run, you need to perform a *breadth and depth analysis*.

Breadth and Depth Analysis

Most developer ecosystems are composed of a few big players and a lot of midsize and small players, as illustrated in Figure 10-1. Consider the following about the mobile ecosystem: you have a few big mobile app developers—Uber, Lyft, Facebook, Supercell, and so forth—as well as many, many other app developers working in smaller companies building mobile apps.

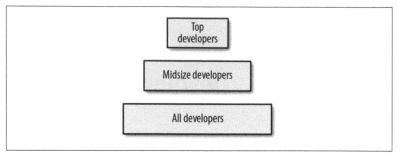

Figure 10-1. Developer tiers

Developers (and hence developer programs) can be categorized along two axes, as shown in Figure 10-2:

Depth axis

The deep developer audience refers to the top partners or top clients that will use your API. You will need to spend more time with these top partners and clients to get them to use it. The programs across this axis deal with few developers, each with a big impact on your ecosystem but high demands on your API.

Breadth axis

The broad developer audience is made up of the midsize and small companies that build on top of your API. It can also include hobbyists and students who are building on your API for nonprofessional reasons. The individual developers across this axis have a small impact on your ecosystem, but together they have a potentially massive impact on your business.

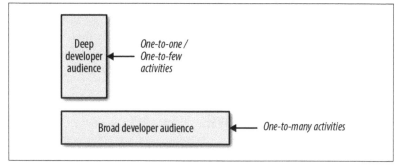

Figure 10-2. Deep and broad developer audiences

The following sections describe developer programs for both audiences in more detail.

Deep Developer Programs

Deep developer programs try to motivate a small group of big clients or partners to use your API. These partners sometimes require a lot of work to engage. Many API and platform providers have a separate team of developer relations experts, called *partner engineers*, that deal with these top partners. Their mission is to work with this key audience to create exemplary large uses of your API.

Let's take a look at some of the kinds of programs that these teams run.

Top Partner Program

The goal of a top partner program is to identify the top users, or potential top users, of your API and to engage with them to build and use your platform. This usually begins with a use case analysis. In this analysis, you list the top use cases of your API and map the top partners for each of them.

For example, suppose that you are building an API to resize, filter, and run other manipulations of images. The API receives an original image, along with transformation parameters, and returns the newly modified image. What are the top use cases that this API might serve? Let's list a few:

Thumbnailing and resizing
Developers of websites should provide their users with thumbnails of their merchandise and let them click the thumbnails to see the larger images.

Watermarks
Developers might like to overlay watermarks on images, either to prevent misuse or to enforce branding.

Mobile optimizations
Mobile developers should compress images for mobile app usage.

There could be many, many more use cases, but let's work with these three for now. For each of these use cases, we list the top developers by market capitalization (market cap) or any other criteria that are important to the business. Table 10-1 shows what this list might look like.

Table 10-1. Top developer partners per target use case

Thumbnailing and resizing	Watermarks	Mobile optimizations
eBay	Getty Images	Snapchat
Amazon	Shutterstock	Instagram
CNN	iStock	Lightroom

The list of partners is usually much larger than this and has more details regarding whether the developer is already using the API, where they are in the funnel, and the impact on the business.

If there are too many use cases that your API can support, you can run a similar analysis but focus on industries rather than use cases. Mapping the top companies per industry can be easier than mapping partners per use case in some instances. Table 10-2 shows how this might look.

Table 10-2. Top developer partners per target industry

Automobile images	Advertising	Social networks
Ford	WPP Group	Facebook
Honda	Omnicom Group	Twitter
Tesla	Dentsu	Snapchat

After mapping your partners by target use case or industries, you need to engage with each of the partners (working together with sales or business development), build a relationship with them, and support these partners in their use of the API. Sometimes these types of activities are called *white-glove* activities, because they are unique for each partner—some partners require a lot of on-site support, some require design or architecture assistance, and others might need to ask a question only once in a while. Because these are one-to-few activities, in which one partner engineer works with a few selected developers, it is easier to fit the activity to the developer's needs.

Beta Program

As you develop your API, you need your top developers to adopt your new functionality, give you feedback on it, and launch with you when you release your new API functionality to the general developer audience, as mentioned in Chapters 4 and 5.

Pro Tip

Launching new features with top developers who are already using them is a common best practice. It shows the entire developer population that these top developers trust and find your new API useful.

If you ever see a keynote address at Google I/O, Facebook F8, or any other big tech event, you will notice that every developer launch is accompanied by a slide or a clip that shows developers already implementing great innovations using the API. This is the result of an early access and partner program.

Here's the way Slack has run this program in the past:

1. **Ideation.** About two months before releasing new API functionality, engineering, product management, marketing, developer relations, and business development gather and think about who their top developers could be. At the end of this stage, they have a list of top developers and the desired use cases they want to implement with those developers.

2. **Recruitment.** Their partner engineering team in developer relations, together with business development, reaches out to partners and asks them to join the beta program for a new feature. The partners are given some mock-ups of the new feature, a pitch about how they might use it, and timelines to launch. At the end of this stage, Slack's team has a list of partners who have committed to the program.

3. **Onboarding.** Each top developer then receives the specification of the new API and a draft of the documentation. This is a raw document created by the content team. At the end of this stage, Slack usually collects feedback from the partners on the specification and feature.

4. **Joint building.** For the next month or so, Slack personnel meet with the top developers on a weekly basis and make sure they are able to solve their problems, fix bugs, and provide feedback on design and implementation. At the end of this stage, they have a set of two to five good integrations and uses of the new API.

5. **Launch prep.** Working with marketing on both sides, Slack coordinates the materials needed for the mutual launch. Slack also publishes a blog post, collects logos and quotes for a press release, and so forth. At the end of this stage, the Slack team ready to launch.

6. **Launch day.** On launch day, Slack's team gathers in a "war room" (or, at Slack, a "peace room") and coordinates (over email and Slack) with partners on when to launch their press releases and their product integrations with Slack's platform.

Running a good beta program not only guarantees a successful set of partners to launch with you but also a better API at launch time. Beta partners are a great way to test, validate the value of, and get feedback on your new API.

Pro Tip

For some developers who sign on, your project may be low priority. This can lead to delays or even cancellations of their participation in the program. To make sure your beta program is successful, it can be helpful to be very hands-on with your beta developers and to have well-defined expectations and well-aligned goals. Be sure to have several partners so as not to have all your eggs in one basket.

Expert Advice

The best APIs are treated like any other product that's important to a business: they're supported, maintained, improved, and altered to fit changing customer needs and expectations. It's important that API teams stay ahead of the demands of their customers and anticipate where new needs are cropping up and where competitive threats are appearing throughout the marketplace. The moment you tell yourself that you've achieved "lock-in" because your customers can't afford to switch away from you is the moment that you've already started to lose.

—Chris Messina, developer experience lead at Uber

Design Sprints

The *design sprint* (*https://www.gv.com/sprint/*) is a process for answering critical product questions through design, prototyping, and testing ideas with developers. Although there are a lot of different things you can do with developers, the design sprint is probably one of our favorites and one of the most effective activities you can do with a top developer trying to figure out "what to build" over your platform or API. We've run many design sprints with top developers at Google and Slack. A design sprint can take a few hours or even a few days. There are books and courses out there that teach about design sprints in detail, but here are the steps at a high level:

Understand
Work with the developer to explain your API's capabilities, and let them teach you about their technologies. Invite business stakeholders who can talk about your mutual business goals, and invite shared users to figure out their key pain points and needs. Bring design, product, and engineering representatives into the room.

Define
Clearly define the problem that you want to tackle. What is the developer's need or pain that you want to address? Do not focus on a solution, just define what the problem is that you want to solve.

Diverge
At this stage, have each member of the design sprint come up with six to eight design solutions for the problem. The idea here is to quietly brainstorm ideas and designs. Participants should encapsulate each idea on a small sticky note that captures the essence.

Decide
Analyze the ideas and decide on the one you want to implement. You can do this by having the group vote for the best idea or through a risk–benefit analysis that compares how difficult each solution is with how valuable is it to the end customer.

Prototype
Spend time prototyping your solution—this can be just mockups, or as high-fidelity as a working prototype. The key here is

to build enough for the end customer to be able to try it out and give feedback.

Validate

Bring in end customers to try out the prototype and provide feedback; bring in internal stakeholders to do this, as well. Capture the feedback, learn, and iterate as needed.

The key benefit of a design sprint is the ability to quickly work together toward a mutual goal. Although design sprints require a lot of time and resources, the outcomes are usually useful because they stem from an actual problem or need and they result in a validated solution.

Pro Tip

Design sprints are also useful because they condense many partner meetings into one.

Broad Developer Programs

Broad developer programs are all about scale (a magical word in Silicon Valley). These programs try to reach as many developers as possible and move them through the funnel discussed in Chapter 8. In contrast to deep programs, the engagement with the developers is not high-touch—no company has the ability to personally support every developer. Broad programs use scalable, low-touch (one-to-many) tools, like videos, docs, events, and code labs, to achieve their targets.

Let's examine a few examples of these types of programs.

Meetups and Community Events

These are probably the most well-known developer relations programs. The goal is to build a community of self-sustaining developers, teaching and supporting one another. Google has one of the biggest developer communities, called Google Developer Groups (GDG), with more than 250 independent groups of developers around the world. Every GDG community meets on a regular basis (usually monthly) and runs evening events where speakers talk about Google technologies. These meetups are the core essence of the community, and community leaders are measured on the meetup cadence. Many communities run hackathons, training days, and big events.

One of the key values of a good community is that it does not require you as the API provider to run each of the meetups. You might need to provide some technical content or food, or give prizes and swag, but you can run hundreds of meetups around the world with as few as one to three full-time community managers. Your community managers scout for new local volunteer community leaders, outline the community's principles (community rules), create community assets (such as a website and training materials for meetups), communicate with each local community to monitor their health, and provide support when needed.

Pro Tip

Not every API requires a separate community of its own. You can offer your content to an existing community, especially if its members would benefit from that content. For example, Unity is a game development platform that might provide tutorials or guides hosted by an Android developer for a community game hackathon.

Hackathons

Hackathons are another very popular and well-known type of developer program. A hackathon is a gathering of developers to brainstorm and develop solutions around a specific topic (e.g., software for healthcare) or technology (e.g., Amazon Alexa skills).

The word *hackathon* is derived from the word *marathon*, but it requires more mental than physical effort. *Hackathons* usually last 24 to 48 hours, during which developers form into groups, decide what to build, prototype, and then present their results to one another at the end of the event.

It is important to be very clear about the structure, time frame, topic, and desired outcome of the hackathon, and to provide the tools for the groups to connect (a spreadsheet of ideas, for example). Many unstructured hackathons fail because people come to the event not knowing what to do, or they spend a lot of time coordinating instead of coding. Hackathons are also expensive in terms of time and resources, so if you do not invite the right people, track signups, and gather product insights, your management might see this effort as a waste of time and money.

Hackathons can be very big, with a lot of API companies working together to help developers innovate. Slack has sponsored a hackathon with 2,000 developers, together with companies such as Lyft, Stripe, Google, Amazon, and Microsoft. Each company provided training materials, engineers to support the hackers, and prizes for the best projects.

Hackathons contribute to developer awareness and proficiency, they connect the API product team and developers at large, and they help collect product feedback and build empathy for developer problems.

Speaking at Events and Event Sponsorships

A lot of companies hire full-time advocates to speak at events around the world. Big companies, like Oracle, Facebook, and Google, run multiday developer events with hundreds of sessions and training seminars. These types of activities are usually effective ways to reach developers at scale because a lot of these sessions are recorded and viewed thousands of times after the event takes place.

Developer events can be very expensive and time-consuming to create if you are a small startup or an independent developer. But if you like to present at third-party events, it is not difficult to find a speaking opportunity at an event that somebody else is hosting.

Pro Tip

Many speaking opportunities come contingent with an event sponsorship agreement, which can be very costly. Make sure you are getting in front of an audience of the right type (developers rather than businesspeople, for example) and size to ensure that you are getting your money's worth. Remember that there are a lot of community events that will be happy to let you speak for free.

Train-the-Trainer and Ambassador Programs

This type of program is called by a different name by each company. For example, Microsoft has its it Microsoft Most Valuable Professional (Microsoft MVP) program, and Google calls it Google Developers Experts. Regardless of the name, the essence of the program is the same: API providers reach out to a set of very proficient members of the developer community and build a special relationship with them so that these developers can become ambassadors within the developer community at large.

Storytime: Google Developers Experts

I started the Google Developers Experts program at Google in a very frugal way—I mapped the top five developers in my region, reached out to them, and told them I wanted to meet. I gathered them all together for dinner, gave them all Google shirts, and told them I would really like to work with them to teach developers how to build on Google technologies. All of them agreed. I then asked my product teams to share presentations, code labs, and training content with my newly formed experts, and asked my experts to use this content to go to events, present, and train developers. We met on a monthly basis for dinner and talk about our progress. I was the only person who actually worked at Google at those dinners, but by far not the most proficient person in Google technologies at the table. We all worked together for a shared goal: to make our developer community awesome.

Today, the Google Developers Experts program is a global program with more than 300 experts around the world. From time to time, I see a person in San Francisco walking proudly in an Expert T-shirt, and I smile to myself.

—Amir Shevat

Online Videos and Streaming

We talked about videos in Chapter 9, but we need to explain the programmatic approach to videos and streaming. Creating a set of videos that explain how to use your API or platform can be a useful practice. Building a program around online content is all about providing developers with an ongoing cadence of content. Google has a show called *(TL;DR) The Developer Show* that resembles a weekly TV show for developers who want to keep up with Google technologies.

Building a high-end video program can be expensive, but you might want to consider using platforms like YouTube or Twitch to do a monthly casual streaming show. In this show, you simply stream yourself building over your API and answer viewers' questions as they come in. For example, Stripe's developer relations team runs a Twitch stream about its payments API and engages with its developers via live chat.

Support, Forums, and Stack Overflow

An important program that is sometimes overlooked is a solid support program, which answers the question, "How do developers get support when they become stuck using your API?"

Slack takes the approach of company-operated support for developers—developers can email questions to *developers@slack.com*, and this opens a Zendesk ticket for Slack's support organization. Slack has a large support team with different product specializations, so these tickets get routed to the developer support team.

Other companies provide online support via forums. Twitch has a very active support forum that enables Twitch employees and community members to answer questions that are raised in the forum.

Another approach is supporting developers on Stack Overflow, an online platform where anyone can ask programming-related questions and find answers. Developers submit questions and other developers answer them. The community moderates the questions and upvotes the answers, creating a high-quality, highly searchable database of questions and answers. The Android developer support program was run on Stack Overflow. They used Stack Overflow's API to retrieve new questions that were relevant to Android development and answered every question.

Credit Program

If your API costs money to use, you might want to consider providing free credits for selected developers. Microsoft, Amazon, and Google all have credit programs for their APIs. Credit programs are usually easy to maintain and track, but they are not useful if your API is free.

Selecting the right developers to give credits to is not easy, and your credits can be abused by the wrong developers. You want to give credits to developers who will convert into paying customers with time. Some companies allocate them to developers based on their company size, while others use startup incubators as a way to distribute the credits to companies that are likely to grow. The key here is that credits are like money: think carefully about who to give them to and what value you are getting back.

Measuring Developer Programs

Determining which programs move which needles in your measurements and how they affect your ecosystem is probably one of the most important activities you can do. Programs might be impactful but can also be useless, and without measurements you will not be able to tell the difference. For each program, you need to understand the following:

- What does this program do?
- What are the expected inputs?
- How is it performing for the expected outcomes?

Table 10-3 presents an example of such measurements for some of the outlined programs.

Table 10-3. Developer programs measurement report

Name	Description	Inputs	Outcomes
Top partner program	Map and drive top partners to build with our API.	Map 15 partners and work with 10 of them this quarter.	Five top partners actively use our API this quarter.
Beta program	Provide feedback on beta features and launch features with partners using our new API capabilities from day one.	Work with seven beta partners to launch feature X.	Capture 10 feature requests and 10 bugs reported by partners. Launch feature X with five partners who use the feature from day one.
Hackathons	Make developers aware of and proficient with our API.	Run five hackathons this quarter.	1,000 developers create an API token during the hackathon.
Speaking at events	Make developers aware of our platform.	Speak at seven big developer events this quarter.	15,000 developers are reached via events or subsequent videos; 5,000 new visitors to our developer site.

As you can see, each program has its own inputs and desired outcomes, and it is easy to mix them up. Some people complain that hackathons are useless because they do not lead to paying customers, but increasing the number of paying customers is not actually the expected outcome of a hackathon. Know what impact you want to have on your ecosystem of developers, and then choose the right program to help you drive that.

Closing Thoughts

There are many other types of programs and subprograms out there, each with different measurements and outcomes. There are also countless new experimental programs that you can run. At Slack and Twitch, we ran a set of developer tours in Europe and Asia in which our entire team would go and meet developers and partners and speak at local events. When building your developer programs, it is important to map the current state and the desired state of your developer ecosystem and then to launch a few experimental programs and see what works for both your developers and your business.

Remember that a developer community is a delicate ecosystem that requires attention and support. Listen to your developers and keep improving your API, resources, and developer programs to fit their needs.

CHAPTER 11

Conclusion

Building a successful API is an art, comprising business analysis, technology architecture, software development, partnership, content writing, developer relations, support, and marketing. It takes a village to build a good, popular API. In this book, we reviewed the best practices and theory for solid API design; we demonstrated a step-by-step practical use case, and we showed you how to build and maintain a developer ecosystem around an API.

One of the important takeaways from this book is to be thoughtful about how you design your API itself and to be considerate of your developer ecosystem.

Among other attributes, a good API:

- Solves an actual developer need or pain point (Chapter 1 and Chapter 8)
- Is consistent (Chapter 7)
- Is stable (Chapter 6)
- Is thoroughly documented (Chapter 9)
- Does not have breaking changes (Chapter 7)
- Has reasonable rate limits (Chapter 6)
- Follows standards (Chapter 2)
- Is reliable and secure (Chapter 3)
- Has a great community and support (Chapter 10)
- Has sample code (Chapter 9)

- Is easy to understand and use (Chapter 4)
- Has a good SDK, in multiple languages (Chapter 6)
- Is easy to test (Chapter 9)

These are not things that just happen, and they are usually difficult and expensive to fix if you get them wrong the first time around. Validate your API with real users; ask your developers for constant feedback; be transparent with your changes, policies, rate limits, and updates; and be a member of your own developer community.

After you unlock the product-market fit for your API and foster a developer ecosystem around it, you will experience magic—developers will use your API to innovate, empower amazing new solutions, and build things you didn't think were possible.

There is no better feeling than building something that millions of people use every day to make their lives better. Trust us, we have done that, and you can, too.

API Design Worksheets

We've added these worksheets to accompany our hands-on design advice. The worksheets can be used to accompany the fictitious example from Chapter 5, or used repeatedly as templates for your own API designs.

Define Business Objectives

The Problem

Briefly define the problem and how it affects customers and the business.

The Impact

Define what success looks like for your API. What will the world be like after you've released your new API?

Key User Stories

List several key user stories for your API with the following template:

> As a **[user type]**, I want **[action]** so that **[outcome]**.

1.
2.
3.
4.
5.

Technology Architecture

Describe the technology architecture you've selected, along with the reasons behind your decision. You may wish to include charts or graphs showing the pros and cons of paradigms you've considered. Here's an optional example table:

Table A-1. Technology architecture

Pattern, paradigm, or protocol considered	Pros	Cons	Selected?

API Specification Template

Title

Authors

Problem

Solution

Implementation

Give a high-level description of the implementation plan. You may wish to use additional tables or diagrams to describe your plan.

Authentication

Describe how developers will gain access to the API.

Other Things We Considered

If you considered any other API paradigms, architectures, authentication strategies, protocols, etc., briefly mention what you considered.

Inputs, Outputs (REST, RPC)

If you're designing a REST or RPC API, describe the endpoints, inputs, and outputs. You may wish to add columns or use a different table format to describe the requests and responses.

Table A-2. Table_name

URI	Inputs	Outputs

Events, Payloads (Event-Driven APIs)

If you're designing an event-driven API, describe the events and their payloads. You may wish to add columns for additional information, such as OAuth scope.

Table A-3. Table_name

Events	Payload

Errors

Table A-4. Technology architecture

HTTP status code	Error code	Verbose error	Description

Feedback Plan

Describe how you plan to gather feedback on your API design, including whether you plan to release to beta testers.

API Implementation Checklist:

❏ Define specific developer problem to solve

❏ Write internal API specification

❏ Get internal feedback on API specification

❏ Build API

    ❏ Authentication

    ❏ Authorization

    ❏ Error handling

    ❏ Rate-limiting

    ❏ Pagination

    ❏ Monitoring and logging

❏ Write documentation

❏ Run beta test with partners on new API

❏ Gather feedback from beta partners and make changes

❏ Create communication plan to notify developers of changes

❏ Release API changes

Index

pros and cons for MyFiles event-
driven API (example), 74

About the Authors

Brenda Jin is an entrepreneur and software engineer. As a staff engineer on the Slack developer platform team, she designed, built, and scaled APIs for third-party developers. As a board member and chapter leader for Girl Develop It, Brenda has contributed to numerous open source teaching materials and empowered thousands of women to learn web and software development.

Saurabh Sahni is a staff engineer on the developer platform team at Slack. For the last eight years, he has been building and designing developer platforms and APIs. Prior to working at Slack, Saurabh led a team of engineers responsible for Yahoo Developer Network infrastructure and developer tools, where he helped launch Yahoo Mobile Developer Suite and several APIs.

Amir Shevat is a VP of developer experience at Twitch. He has spent the past 15 years building developer products, APIs, and ecosystems around APIs at Slack, Microsoft, and Google. He is also the author of *Designing Bots* (O'Reilly).

Colophon

The animal on the cover of *Designing Web APIs* is the Cozumel fox, an undescribed species of the genus *Urocyon*. About a third of the size of the gray fox, these canids are native to Cozumel Island, Mexico, where they have lived exclusively since at least the times of the Mayan civilization. The last confirmed sighting of a Cozumel fox was in 2001; it may already be extinct, but formal investigations have not been conducted.

Many of the animals on O'Reilly covers are endangered; all of them are important to the world. To learn more about how you can help, go to *animals.oreilly.com*.

The cover image is from Beverley Tucker's *General Report upon The Zoology of the Several Pacific Railroad Routes*. The cover fonts are URW Typewriter and Guardian Sans. The text font is Adobe Minion Pro; the heading font is Adobe Myriad Condensed; and the code font is Dalton Maag's Ubuntu Mono.

Learn from experts.
Find the answers you need.

Sign up for a **10-day free trial** to get **unlimited access** to all of the content on Safari, including Learning Paths, interactive tutorials, and curated playlists that draw from thousands of ebooks and training videos on a wide range of topics, including data, design, DevOps, management, business—and much more.

Start your free trial at:
oreilly.com/safari

(No credit card required.)